Microsoft® Office Access 2003: Quick Course 1 of 2

Microsoft Office Access 2003: Quick Course 1 of 2

MICHELLE MAROTTI
DeKalb Technical College

BRIAN FAVRO
Labyrinth Publications

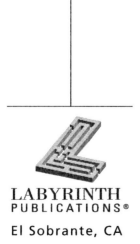

LABYRINTH
PUBLICATIONS®
El Sobrante, CA

Microsoft Office Access 2003: Quick Course 1
by Michelle Marotti and Brian Favro

Copyright © 2004 by Labyrinth Publications

LABYRINTH
PUBLICATIONS®

Labyrinth Publications
P.O. Box 20820
El Sobrante, California 94803
800.522.9746
On the Web at labpub.com

President and Publisher:
Brian Favro

Series Editor:
Russel Stolins

Managing Editor:
Laura A. Lionello

Production Manager:
Rad Proctor

Editorial/Production Team:
Holly Hammond, Nancy Logan,
Nancy Roberts

Indexing: Joanne Sprott

Cover and Interior Design:
Seventeenth Street Studios

ISBN 1-59136-039-0

Manufactured in the United States of America.

19 18 17 16 15 14   R

Microsoft Office Access 2003: Quick Course 1

Microsoft Office Specialist Program

What Does This Logo Mean?

⚠NOTE!

To be fully prepared for the Microsoft Office Access 2003 exam, complete both Quick Courses: Microsoft Office Access 2003: Quick Course 1 and Microsoft Office Access 2003: Quick Course 2.

It means this courseware has been approved by the Microsoft® Office Specialist program to be among the finest available for learning Access 2003. It also means that upon completion of this courseware, you may be prepared to become a Microsoft Office Specialist.

What Is a Microsoft Office Specialist?

A Microsoft Office Specialist is an individual who has certified skills in one or more Microsoft Office desktop applications such as Microsoft Word, Microsoft Excel, Microsoft Access, Microsoft PowerPoint®, or Microsoft Project. The Microsoft Office Specialist program typically offers certification exams at different skill levels.* The Microsoft Office Specialist program is the only Microsoft-approved program in the world for certifying proficiency in Microsoft Office desktop applications and Microsoft Project. This certification can be a valuable asset in any job search or career advancement.

Which Exam(s) Will This Publication Prepare You to Take?

Microsoft Office Access 2003: Quick Course 1 and *Microsoft Office Access 2003: Quick Course 2*, used in combination, have been approved by Microsoft as courseware for the Microsoft Office Specialist program. After completing a two-course sequence, students will be prepared to take the Microsoft Office Access 2003 exam.

For more information:

■ To learn more about becoming a Microsoft Office Specialist, visit www.microsoft.com/officespecialist/.

■ To purchase a Microsoft Office Specialist certification exam, visit www.microsoft.com/officespecialist/.

■ To learn about other Microsoft Office Specialist approved courseware from Labyrinth Publications, visit labpub.com/mos/.

---

* The availability of Microsoft Office Specialist certification exams varies by application, application version, and language. Visit www.microsoft.com/officespecialist/ for exam availability.

Microsoft, the Microsoft Office Specialist logo, PowerPoint, and Outlook are either registered trademarks or trademarks of Microsoft Corporation in the United States and/or other countries.

Microsoft Office Access 2003 objectives covered in this book

Objective Number	Skill Sets and Skills	Concept Page References	Exercise Page References
AC03S-1-1	Create Access databases	5–6	6–7, 26
AC03S-1-2	Create and modify tables	8, 34, 41	10–13, 23, 25, 34–36, 42–44
AC03S-1-3	Define and modify field types	9–10, 50	50–52
AC03S-1-4	Modify field properties	44–45	45–47
AC03S-1-5	Create and modify one-to-many relationships	118	119–120, 141–142
AC03S-1-6	Enforce referential integrity	119	121
AC03S-1-7	Create and modify queries	133–134	130–131, 133–135, 151–153
AC03S-1-8	Create forms	64, 69	65, 70, 78, 80
AC03S-1-10	Create reports	71	72–75, 81–82, 147–148
AC03S-2-1	Enter, edit, and delete records	16	16–18
AC03S-2-2	Find and move among records	36–37, 65	37–39, 66–67
AC03S-3-1	Create and modify calculated fields and aggregate functions	123–124, 127	124–125, 127–128, 143–145, 149
AC03S-3-4	Format datasheets	20, 107	20–21, 108
AC03S-3-5	Sort records	95, 97	96–98
AC03S-3-6	Filter records	40	40–41
AC03S-4-2	View objects and object data in other views	19	19
AC03S-4-3	Print database objects and data	18–19	21, 25

Contents in Brief

Contents

Index of Quick Reference Tables

List of Keyboard Shortcuts

Editing Commands

[Ctrl]+[C] to copy

[Ctrl]+[V] to paste

Design Commands

[Ctrl]+[Enter] to open selected object in Design view

[Ctrl]+[S] to save open object

[Delete] to delete selected object

[Enter] to open selected object

[F2] to edit object name

[F6] to go back to Field Descriptor area

[F6] to go to Field Properties area

Document Commands

[Ctrl]+[P] to display Print dialog box

Preface

Microsoft Office Access 2003: Quick Course 1 enables students to master the fundamental skills required for effective use of Microsoft Access 2003. When used as part of a two-book sequence with *Microsoft Office Access 2003: Quick Course 2*, it also prepares students to pass the Microsoft Office Access 2003 exam.

The focus of *Microsoft Office Access 2003: Quick Course 1* is basic skills. The text leverages Labyrinth's renowned ease-of-understanding expertise in introducing basic Access skills through creative case studies. Topics covered include setting up a new database, entering data, querying the database, and generating reports. Students develop sophisticated databases that build from lesson-to-lesson. This book assumes that students understand the basic concepts of using a mouse and drop-down menus, saving files to some type of storage media, and other basic skills required to run Windows programs. Upon completion of this course, students will be prepared for the subject matter and challenges found in the Level 2 Quick Course.

Over the last 10 years of writing and publishing Microsoft Office courses, Labyrinth has developed a unique instructional design that makes learning faster and easier for students at all skill levels. Teachers have found that the Labyrinth model provides effective learning for students in both self-paced and instructor-led learning environments. The material is carefully written and built around compelling case studies that demonstrate the relevance of all subject matter. Mastery of subject matter is ensured through the use of multiple levels of carefully crafted exercises. The text includes Concepts Review questions and Hands-On, Skill Builder, Assessment, and Critical Thinking exercises.

The course is also supported on the Labyrinth Website with a comprehensive instructor support package that includes a printable solutions guide, detailed lesson plans, PowerPoint presentations, a course syllabus, extensive test banks, and more.

We are grateful to the many teachers who have used Labyrinth titles and suggested improvements to us during the 10 years we have been writing and publishing Office books.

About the Authors

Michelle Marotti (BS, Computer Science; MS, Education) earned her degrees from Southern Oregon University. While at Southern Oregon, she began teaching seminars for Word, Excel, and Access, helping the staff migrate to these new applications. After receiving her teaching certificate, she went on to teach high school computer classes. Since June of 2000, she has taught at DeKalb Technical College near Atlanta, Georgia, as a computer instructor. Michelle is coauthor of *Microsoft Office 2003: Essentials Course*.

Brian Favro (BSc, Computer Engineering) began teaching adult education classes in Richmond, California, in 1991. He found that few books on computer applications met the needs of students and began writing materials to meet those needs. From this experience, he launched Labyrinth Publications and developed the "ease of understanding" format that evolved, with the help of Russel Stolins, into the instructional model that makes Labyrinth books so unique. Other instructors liked what he was doing and soon Brian was selling his books to them, and Labyrinth Publications was born.

Introduction

Welcome to Labyrinth Publications, where you'll find your course to success. Our real world, project-based approach to education helps students grasp concepts, not just read about them, and prepares them for success in the workplace. Our straightforward, easy-to-follow language is ideal for both instructor-led classes and self-paced labs. At Labyrinth, we're dedicated to one purpose: delivering quality courseware that is comprehensive yet concise, effective, and affordable. It's no wonder that Labyrinth is a recognized leader in Microsoft Office and operating system courseware.

More than a million users have learned Office our way. At Labyrinth, we believe that successful teaching begins with exceptional courseware. That's why we've made it our goal to develop innovative texts that empower both teachers and students. We give educators the necessary resources to deliver clear, relevant instruction and students the power to take their new skills far beyond the classroom.

Labyrinth Series Give You More Choices

Labyrinth offers seven exceptionally priced series to meet your needs:

- Microsoft Office 2003 Series—These full-length, full-featured texts explore applications in the Office 2003 system. All application-specific books in this series are Microsoft Office Specialist approved for the Microsoft Office 2003 certification exams, and the Word and Excel books are also approved for the Microsoft Office 2003 Expert certification exams.

- Silver™ Series—Designed especially for adult learners, seniors, and non-native speakers, this series includes larger fonts and screens, our unmistakable straightforward design, and fun hands-on projects.

- ProStart Foundations™ Series—These full-length, full-featured texts for operating systems and applications include the new Microsoft Windows titles and are designed to lay a solid foundation for students.

- ProStart™ Series for Office XP—These full-length, full-featured texts walk students through the basic and advanced skills of the primary Office XP applications. Most are Microsoft Office Specialist approved. The Office XP Essentials and Comprehensive courses offer surveys of all the primary Office XP applications.

- Briefcase™ Series for Office XP—The popular and inexpensive choice for short classes, self-paced courses, and accelerated workshops (or mix and match for longer classes), these concise texts provide quick access to key concepts. Most are Microsoft Office Specialist approved.

- Off to Work™ Series for Office 2000—Full-length, full-featured texts set the standard for clarity and ease of use in this series. All books in this series are Microsoft Office Specialist approved.

- Briefcase Series for Office 2000—Designed for short classes, self-paced courses, and accelerated workshops, each lesson in this series is broken down into subtopics that provide quick access to key concepts. All books in this series are Microsoft Office Specialist approved.

Microsoft Office 2003 Series Teaching Resources

Instructor Support Material

To help you be more successful, Labyrinth provides a comprehensive instructor support package that includes the following:

Teaching Tools

- Detailed lesson plans, including a topic sequence and suggested classroom demonstrations

- PowerPoint presentations that give an overview of key concepts for each lesson (also available online for students)

- Answer keys for the Concepts Review questions in each lesson

- Comprehensive classroom setup instructions

- A customizable sample syllabus

- A teacher-customizable background knowledge survey to gather information on student needs and experience at the beginning of the course

Testing Tools

- Printer-friendly exercise solution guides and solution files for Hands-On, Skill Builder, Assessment, and Critical Thinking exercises

- Teacher-customizable, project-based Assessment exercises

- Teacher-customizable test banks of objective questions for each lesson and unit

- TestComposer™ test generator for editing test banks with Microsoft Word (and for creating new question banks and online tests)

These resources are available on our Website at labpub.com and on our instructor support CD, which you can obtain by calling our customer service staff at 800.522.9746.

Website

The Website labpub.com/learn/access03/ features content designed to support the lessons and provide additional learning resources for this book. This main page contains links to individual lesson pages. Some of the items you will find at this site are described below.

PowerPoint Presentations The same presentations available to instructors are accessible online. They make excellent tools for review, particularly for students who miss a class session.

Downloads Required course files can be downloaded on the lesson pages.

Student Exercise Files The student files needed to complete certain Hands-On, Skill Builder, Assessment, and Critical Thinking exercises are available for download at labpub.com/students/fdbc2003.asp.

Labyrinth's Successful Instructional Design

In conjunction with our straightforward writing style, Labyrinth books feature a proven instructional design. The following pages point out the carefully crafted design elements that build student confidence and ensure success.

Lesson introductions present clear learning objectives.

Case studies introduce a practical application that integrates topics presented in each lesson.

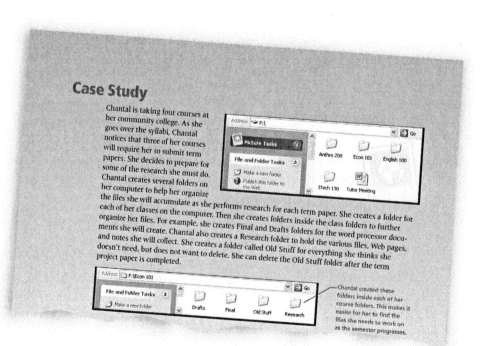

Concepts discussions are kept concise and use illustrations for added clarity and to help students understand the material introduced.

Quick Reference tables provide generic procedures for key tasks that work outside the context of the lesson.

Hands-On exercises are detailed tutorials that help students master the skills introduced in the concepts discussions. The illustrations provide clear instruction and allow unparalleled ease of use.

The Help Window Toolbar

You will encounter this toolbar when viewing Help topics in the Microsoft Word Help Window.

The Auto Tile button displays the Word window and the Help window tiled. If the window is already tiled, the button name changes to Untile. Clicking it causes the Help window to float over the Word window.

Move back one topic.
Move forward one topic.
Print the topic.

QUICK REFERENCE: MOUSE MOTIONS

Motion	How to Do It	This motion is used...
Click	Gently tap and immediately to release the left mouse button.	to "press" a button or select a menu option or object on the screen.
Double-click	Click twice in rapid succession.	as a shortcut for many types of common commands.
Drag	Press and hold down the left mouse button while sliding the mouse. Release the mouse button when you reach your destination.	to move an object, select several objects, draw lines, and select text.
Right-click	Gently tap and immediately release the right mouse button.	to display a context-sensitive menu for the object at which you are pointing.
Point	Slide the mouse without pressing a button until the pointer is in the desired location.	to position the pointer before using one of the four motions above, to select an object on the screen, or to get a menu to appear.

Hands-On 2.7 Move and Size the WordPad Window

In this exercise, you will move the WordPad window to a different location on the Desktop, then change the size of the window.

1. Follow these steps to move the WordPad window:

Ⓐ Click the Save in drop-down list, and choose the 3½ Floppy (A:) drive.

Ⓑ Notice that WordPad proposes the name Document (or Document.doc) in the filename field.

Ⓒ The Hibernation option replaces Stand By in the Windows XP **shutdown** window when you press the ⟨SHIFT⟩ key.

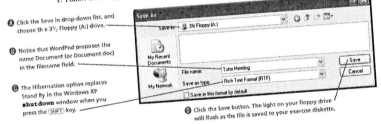

Ⓓ Click the Save button. The light on your floppy drive will flash as the file is saved to your exercise diskette.

122 Lesson 2: Working with Windows Programs

The Concepts Review section at the end of each lesson includes both true/false and multiple choice questions.

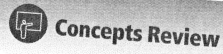

Concepts Review

True/False Questions

1. A Contents (or Home in Windows XP) search of online Help lets you locate Help topics by typing keywords.

2. A My Computer window lets you view the files and folders on the computer.   TRUE   FALSE

3. Windows organizes drives and folders in a hierarchy.   TRUE   FALSE

4. You can use the (CTRL) key to randomly select a group of files.   TRUE   FALSE

5. Folders can have subfolders within them.   TRUE   FALSE

6. You can use the Cut and Paste commands to move files.   TRUE   FALSE

7. Files are sent to the Recycle Bin when they are deleted from floppy disks.   TRUE   FALSE

8. The Properties command displays how much space is left on a floppy disk.   TRUE   FALSE

9. An Exploring window gives you a two-panel view of files and folder.   TRUE   FALSE

10. A quick way to open a file is to double-click on it in a My Computer windows.   TRUE   FALSE

Multiple Choice Questions

1. Which of the following methods would you use to view files and folders on the computer:
   a. Open a My Computer Window

3. Which command is used to create a new folder?
   a. File→Folder→Create
   b. File→New→Folder

Skill Builders, Assessments, and Critical Thinking exercises provide fun, hands-on projects with reduced levels of detailed instruction so students can develop and test their mastery of the material.

Skill Builders

Skill Builder 3.1   Work with Online Help

In this exercise, you will practice looking up various topics in Windows' online Help.

1. Click the [start] button and choose Help from the Start Window.

Assessments

Assessment 3.1   Edit a Document

In this exercise, you will edit a document that is marked up for changes.

the Standard toolbar.

click on Maine.   ...ntains formatting that you

Critical Thinking

Critical Thinking 3.1   On Your Own

Compose a new letter to Donna Wilson using the AutoCorrect shortcut you just created. Request that Donna send you information on Citizen Bank's new Small Business Credit Line program. Let Donna know that because you are starting a new business venture (you choose the venture), you are interested in obtaining financing from the bank. Save the letter as **Wilson Letter 2** then close it.

How This Book Is Organized

The information in this book is presented so that you master the fundamental skills first, and then build on those skills as you work with the more comprehensive topics.

Visual Conventions

This book uses many visual and typographic cues to guide you through the lessons. This page provides examples and describes the function of each cue.

Type this text   Anything you should type at the keyboard is printed in this typeface.

    Tips, Notes, and Warnings are used throughout the text to draw attention to certain topics.

Command→Command   This convention indicates multiple selections to be made from a menu bar. For example, File→Save means to select File, and then to select Save.

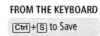   These margin notes indicate shortcut keys for executing a task described in the text.

    Quick Reference tables provide generic instructions for key tasks. Only perform these tasks if you are instructed to in an exercise.

    Hands-On exercises are introduced immediately after concept discussions. They provide detailed, step-by-step tutorials so you can master the skills presented.

Concepts discussions that deal with the Microsoft Office Specialist Program exam objectives are marked with one of these icons.

    The Concepts Review section includes both true/false and multiple choice questions designed to gauge your understanding of concepts.

    Skill Builder exercises provide additional hands-on practice with moderate assistance.

    Assessment exercises test your skills by describing the correct results without providing specific instructions on how to achieve them.

    Critical Thinking exercises are the most challenging. They provide general instructions, allowing you to use your skills and creativity to achieve the result you envision.

Microsoft Office Access 2003: Quick Course 1

LESSON 1

Creating Tables and Entering Data

Rick Cunningham
Jerry Maag

In this lesson, you will begin
developing a database for
the Pinnacle Pet Care clinic.
You will set up one Access
table and enter data in it.
All data in an Access database
is stored in tables. You will
learn how to widen table
columns, change the margins
and page orientation, and print
the contents of tables. The
Pinnacle Pet Care database will
continue to be developed in
later lessons.

Microsoft Office Access 2003 objectives covered in this lesson

Objective Number	Skill Sets and Skills	Concept Page References	Exercise Page References
AC03S-1-1	Create Access databases	5–6	6–7, 26
AC03S-1-2	Create and modify tables	8	10–13, 23, 25
AC03S-1-3	Define and modify field types	9–10	
AC03S-2-1	Enter, edit, and delete records	16	16–18
AC03S-3-4	Format datasheets	20	20–21
AC03S-4-2	View objects and object data in other views	19	19
AC03S-4-3	Print database objects and data	18–19	21, 25

Additional learning resources are available at labpub.com/learn/access03/

Case Study

Al Smith is a veterinarian and owner of the Pinnacle Pet Care clinic. Al recently contracted with Penny Johnson, a freelance programmer and Microsoft Access database developer, to develop an order entry system using Access 2003. Al wants to improve customer service by giving the office staff instant access to customer account information. Al chooses Access as his database tool because of its customization capabilities and its integration with other Office applications. Al hopes Access and the other Office applications will make Pinnacle Pet Care's customer service equitable to the excellent care provided to pets.

You can use forms to enter data into tables and to display records.

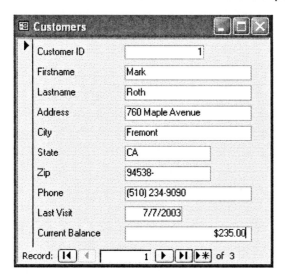

In Access, all data is stored in tables.

Customer ID	Firstname	Lastname	Address	City	State	Zip	Phone	Last Visit	Current Balance
1	Mark	Roth	760 Maple Avenue	Fremont	CA	94538-	(510) 234-9090	7/7/2003	$235.00
2	Tony	Simpson	312 York Lane	Richmond	CA	94804-	(510) 238-2233	9/7/2003	$185.00
3	Jason	Jones	2233 Crystal Street	San Mateo	CA	94403-	(415) 312-2312	7/15/2003	$48.00

You can create reports using data from your tables.

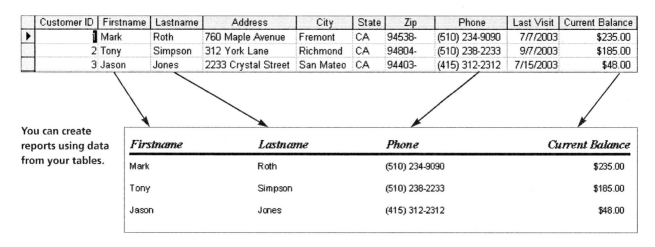

Firstname	Lastname	Phone	Current Balance
Mark	Roth	(510) 234-9090	$235.00
Tony	Simpson	(510) 238-2233	$185.00
Jason	Jones	(415) 312-2312	$48.00

3

Introducing Access

A database is a collection of information. Microsoft Access is a relational database management system that lets you store, organize, and manage information such as customers, products, employees, and projects. Access is a powerful and flexible program that can handle virtually any data management task. For example, you can use Access to keep a simple contact list or you can develop a full-featured order entry and database management system. Access gives anyone with a personal computer the ability to organize and manage data in a sophisticated manner.

Access is an integral part of the Office 2003 suite of software tools because it is the data storage and management tool. You can share Access data with Word, Excel, PowerPoint, and Outlook. For example, you can merge a Word form letter with an Access database to produce a mass mailing. You can also export Access data to Excel then use Excel's calculating and charting capabilities to analyze the data.

 ## Starting Access

In older versions of Windows, the command on the Start Menu is Programs. This text will use (All) Programs to cover all versions of Windows.

The method you use to start Access depends on whether you intend to create a new database or use an existing database. If you are creating a new database, use one of the following methods to start Access:

- Click the **start** button and choose Microsoft Access from the (All) Programs menu.
- Click the **start** button, choose New Office Document, choose the General tab, and double-click the Blank Database icon.

Once Access is started, you can create a new database by choosing the Create a New File option in the Task Pane then choosing the Blank Database option. Access will prompt you to save the new database and give it a name. Name the file at this time because you won't be given the option again.

Use one of the following methods if you intend to open an existing Access database:

- Navigate to the desired database using Windows Explorer or My Computer and double-click the database.
- Click the **start** button and choose Microsoft Access from the (All) Programs menu.

Once Access is started, you may see the file you intend to open listed under Open on the task pane. If you don't, you can open an existing file by choosing the More option and navigating to the desired file.

 ## Hands-On 1.1   Start Access

In this exercise, you will start the Access program.

1. Start your computer and the Windows Desktop will appear.

2. Click the **start** button and choose (All) Programs.

3. Choose Microsoft Access from the (All) Programs menu.
   Access will start and the Access window will appear.

Creating a New Database

You can create a new, blank Access database from scratch or you can use Access's Database Wizard to help you build a database. The task pane that appears on the right side of the Access window gives you several choices. The task pane can be displayed or hidden using the View→Task Pane command.

You open a recently used database or search for an existing database using this section of the task pane.

You create a new database using this section.

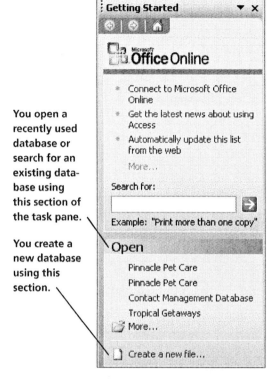

You can create a blank database, a data Access page, or a project using this section of the task pane.

If you choose the On My Computer option then choose one of Access' built-in database templates, the Database Wizard is initiated and guides you step-by-step through the creation of a new database.

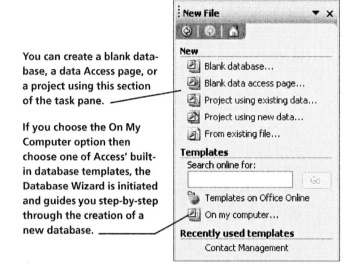

The Database Wizard

The Database Wizard lets you choose one of Access's built-in database templates as the basis for your new database. The Database Wizard takes you step-by-step through a series of screens that lets you customize a built-in template to suit your needs. The resulting database is often sufficient to meet the needs of most individuals and some small businesses and organizations. A database created with the wizard can also be used as a foundation from which a more sophisticated database can be developed.

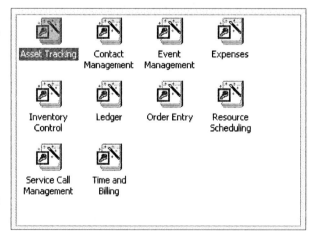

Built-in database templates

Working with Blank Databases

You can also start with a blank database and add objects to it as needed. An Access database is composed of various objects including tables, queries, forms, and reports. Each object type can be created from scratch using a Design view for the particular type of object. Access also provides wizards to help you set up individual objects. You will use both of these techniques as you develop the Pinnacle Pet Care database throughout this course.

Understanding Database Design

The first step in designing any database is to determine the type of information you will need to keep in your database. Examples of data include the name, address, telephone number, and email address of customers or contacts. Once the needed information has been determined, you can design the database to accommodate it. A database structure can be changed but it is more complicated after data has been entered. Sometimes changing the structure can corrupt or delete data that has already been entered. That is why it is important to begin with a good design.

Storing Your Exercise Files

Throughout this book you will be referred to files in your "file storage location." You can store your exercise files on various media such as a floppy disk, a USB flash drive, the My Documents folder, or on a network drive at a school or company. While many figures in the exercises may display files in the 3½ Floppy (A:) drive, it is assumed that you will substitute your own location for that shown in the figure. See the appendix for additional information on alternative file storage media.

The Save In box as it appears in the book

The Save In box as it might appear if you are saving your files to a USB flash drive

 Hands-On 1.2   Create a Blank Database

In this exercise, you will create a new Access database and explore its components.

Before You Begin: If you have not done so already, please turn to Downloading the Student Exercise Files section of the appendix (page 161) for instructions on how to retrieve the student exercise files for this book from the Labyrinth Website, and to copy the files to your file storage location for use in this and future lessons. See also pages 163–167 for additional details about using this book with a floppy disk, USB flash drive, the My Documents folder, and a folder on a network drive.

1. Make sure the task pane is displayed on the right side of the Access window. If it isn't, use the View→Task Pane command to display it.

2. Choose the Create a New File option.

3. Choose the Blank Database option and notice that the File New Database box appears.

4. Follow these steps to save the new database to your file storage location:

Ⓐ Click here and choose your file storage location. It is most likely the 3½ Floppy (A:) drive.

Ⓑ Notice that Access proposes a name, such as db1, in the File Name box.

Ⓒ Type the name **Pinnacle Pet Care** to replace the proposed name. (If you switched disk drives then you may need to click in the File Name box, delete the name in the box with the `Delete` or `Backspace` keys and type the new name.)

Ⓓ Click the Create button.

5. Follow these steps to explore the Access database window:

Ⓐ Notice the various object buttons displayed on the Objects bar. An Access database is composed of objects. You can create new objects in Design view or with wizards by choosing one of the Create options displayed in the window. Objects you create are also displayed in the database window.

Ⓑ Try clicking the various object buttons.

Ⓒ Click the Tables button when you have finished exploring.

Notice the title bar in the preceding illustration. The text on your title bar may differ; do not be concerned with this.

Introducing Access Tables

In Access, data are stored in tables. Tables organize data so that it can easily be output at a later time. A simple database may have one or two tables while a sophisticated database may have dozens or even hundreds of tables. A separate table is used for each type of related data. For example, your Pinnacle Pet Care database will initially have a table for customers and a table for pets.

Records

Tables are composed of rows and each row is known as a record. For example, your Pinnacle Pet Care database will have a Customers table that stores all of the customer information. All information for one customer is a record. You will have as many records in your database as you have customers.

Fields

Each record is divided into fields. A record can have many fields. For example, the Customers table will have fields for the Customer ID, name, address, telephone number, etc. In Access, each column in a table is a field. Take a few moments to study the following illustration, which shows the first two tables you will create in the Pinnacle Pet Care database.

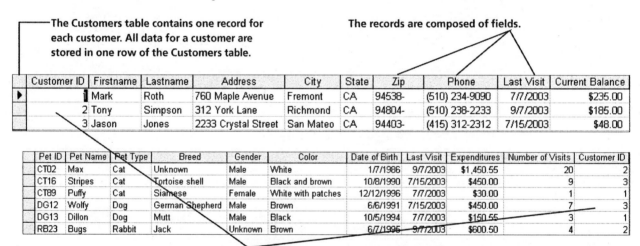

The Customers table contains one record for each customer. All data for a customer are stored in one row of the Customers table.

The records are composed of fields.

Customer ID	Firstname	Lastname	Address	City	State	Zip	Phone	Last Visit	Current Balance
1	Mark	Roth	760 Maple Avenue	Fremont	CA	94538-	(510) 234-9090	7/7/2003	$235.00
2	Tony	Simpson	312 York Lane	Richmond	CA	94804-	(510) 238-2233	9/7/2003	$185.00
3	Jason	Jones	2233 Crystal Street	San Mateo	CA	94403-	(415) 312-2312	7/15/2003	$48.00

Pet ID	Pet Name	Pet Type	Breed	Gender	Color	Date of Birth	Last Visit	Expenditures	Number of Visits	Customer ID
CT02	Max	Cat	Unknown	Male	White	1/7/1986	9/7/2003	$1,450.55	20	2
CT16	Stripes	Cat	Tortoise shell	Male	Black and brown	10/8/1990	7/15/2003	$450.00	9	3
CT89	Puffy	Cat	Siamese	Female	White with patches	12/12/1996	7/7/2003	$30.00	1	1
DG12	Wolfy	Dog	German Shepherd	Male	Brown	6/6/1991	7/15/2003	$450.00	7	3
DG13	Dillon	Dog	Mutt	Male	Black	10/5/1994	7/7/2003	$150.55	3	1
RB23	Bugs	Rabbit	Jack	Unknown	Brown	6/7/1995	9/7/2003	$600.50	4	2

Notice that the Customer ID field appears in both the Customers and Pets tables. Eventually, this field will be used to establish a relationship between the two tables. Establishing relationships between tables is what gives Access and other relational database systems their power and flexibility.

Working with Table Structure

In Access, you can set up tables in Design view or with the Table Wizard. In Design view, you specify the field names, the data type of each field, and any other parameters as needed. Design view lets you precisely determine the characteristics of each field. The Table Wizard automates the process of creating a table by letting you choose from a set of predefined fields. The Table Wizard lacks the flexibility of Design view; however, it is often useful to beginning Access users. Besides, you can always switch to Design view to modify a table that has been set up with the Table Wizard. Access gives you complete control in setting up and modifying tables and other Access objects.

Field Names

Each field in an Access table is identified by a unique name. The name can be up to 64 characters in length and can contain letters, numbers, spaces, and most punctuation marks. Field names cannot contain periods, exclamation marks, or square brackets [ ]. Some examples of field names from the Pinnacle Pet Care Customers table are Firstname, Lastname, Address, City, State, and Zip.

Data Types

Each field is assigned a data type that determines the type of data the field may contain. The most common data types are text, number, currency, and date/time.

- Text—Text fields can contain any type of character. The default size of text fields is 50 characters; however, you can increase or decrease the size as desired.

- Number—Number fields can only contain numbers and typically used in calculations. Therefore, you should use the Text data type if a field will contain a combination of text and numbers or if you are entering phone numbers or zip codes.

- Currency—Currency fields can be used in calculations. Access formats the numbers in a currency field with dollar signs, commas, decimal points, and digits following the decimal point.

- Date/Time—Date/Time fields can contain dates and times. Dates can be used in calculations. For example, you can subtract two dates to determine the number of days between the dates.

- Memo—Memo fields can hold up to 65,536 characters. Use this field when you need to enter lengthy text such as comments or notes.

- AutoNumber—AutoNumber assigns an automatic sequential number to each record. This works well for something like a customer or account number. Using this data type will ensure that no two records have the same number.

- Yes/No—Yes/No fields can contain only one of two values; for example Yes/No, On/Off, or True/False.

- OLE Object—OLE object fields are used to store pictures, sound clips, other documents, or spreadsheets.

- Hyperlink—Hyperlinks are links to another location, such as the Web or another file.

- List—The List field brings up a wizard that walks you through setting up a field that contains list items. It helps you create a drop-down list from which the user can pick. Use this data type when there are certain values that should be entered into the field; for example, a part number or a day of the week.

Field Properties

Each data type has several field properties that can be used to customize the field. For example, you can change the Field Size property for text fields to increase or decrease the maximum number of characters allowed in the field. The field properties can be modified for each field in a table when the table is displayed in Design view.

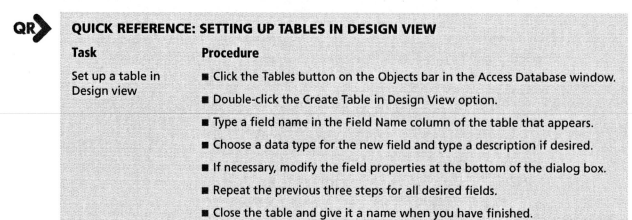

QR QUICK REFERENCE: SETTING UP TABLES IN DESIGN VIEW

Task	Procedure
Set up a table in Design view	■ Click the Tables button on the Objects bar in the Access Database window.
	■ Double-click the Create Table in Design View option.
	■ Type a field name in the Field Name column of the table that appears.
	■ Choose a data type for the new field and type a description if desired.
	■ If necessary, modify the field properties at the bottom of the dialog box.
	■ Repeat the previous three steps for all desired fields.
	■ Close the table and give it a name when you have finished.

 Hands-On 1.3   Set Up a Table in Design View

FROM THE KEYBOARD
[F6] to go to Field Properties area
[F6] to go back to Field Descriptor area

In this exercise, you will begin setting up the Pets table for the Pinnacle Pet Care database.

Define Text Fields

1. Follow these steps to display a new table in Design view:

Ⓐ Make sure the Tables button is chosen on the Objects bar.

Ⓑ Double-click the Create Table in Design View option.

2. If necessary, maximize 🔲 both the Access program window and the Table Design window within the Access window.

3. Follow these steps to define a text field:

(A) Type **Pet ID** as the field name.

(B) Tap the [Tab] key to move to the Data Type box. Notice the Data Type is set to Text. This is correct because the Pet ID will be composed of letters and numbers. The Text data type is used if the field contains text or a combination of text and numbers.

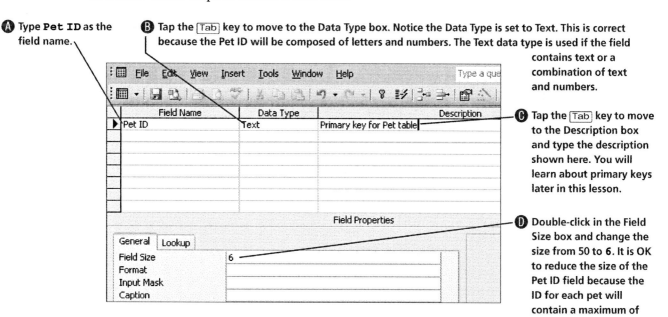

(C) Tap the [Tab] key to move to the Description box and type the description shown here. You will learn about primary keys later in this lesson.

(D) Double-click in the Field Size box and change the size from 50 to **6**. It is OK to reduce the size of the Pet ID field because the ID for each pet will contain a maximum of six characters. The Field Properties section of the dialog box reflects the properties of the current field (Pet ID). You will learn more about these properties as you progress through this course.

You have just defined a field in your database. You will enter data into this field and other fields later in this lesson. You will use a data entry mode known as Datasheet view to enter the data. Currently, you are working in Design view, which allows you to define a table. The Text field type that you chose for the Pet ID field will allow you to enter any type of data in the field. However, the Pet ID for each pet will be restricted to six characters.

4. Follow these steps to define another text field:

(A) Click in the next Field Name box and type **Pet Name**. The Pet Name field will contain the names of the pets.

(B) Tap the [Tab] key and Text will appear as the default Data Type. Leave the Data Type set to Text and do not enter a description for this field. Descriptions are optional and are only used when necessary.

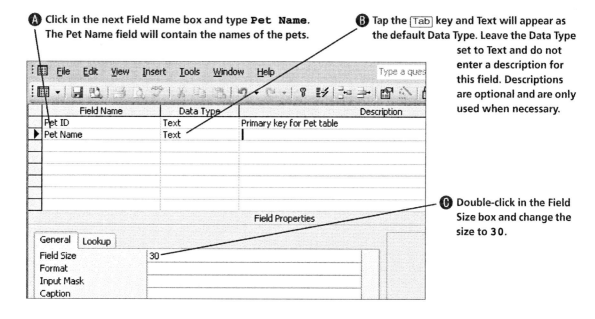

(C) Double-click in the Field Size box and change the size to **30**.

5. Follow the same procedure you used in step 4 to create the next four fields shown in the following illustration. Set the Field Size to **30** for all of the fields except the Gender field. Set the size of the Gender field to **10**.

Field Name	Data Type	Description
Pet ID	Text	Primary key for Pet table
Pet Name	Text	
▶ Pet Type	Text	
Breed	Text	
Gender	Text	
Color	Text	

Define Date Fields

In the next few steps, you will define two fields that will eventually contain dates. You will set the Data Type to Date/Time for these fields. This is useful because Access will identify the contents of the fields as dates. Dates can be used in calculations. For example, you can have Access calculate the number of days an account is past due by subtracting the invoice date from the current date.

6. Follow these steps to define a date field:

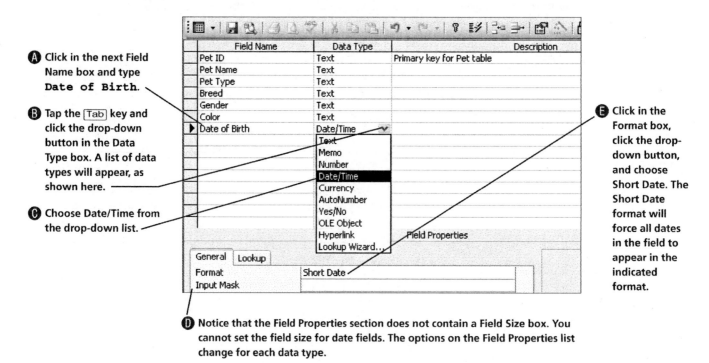

A Click in the next Field Name box and type **Date of Birth**.

B Tap the [Tab] key and click the drop-down button in the Data Type box. A list of data types will appear, as shown here.

C Choose Date/Time from the drop-down list.

E Click in the Format box, click the drop-down button, and choose Short Date. The Short Date format will force all dates in the field to appear in the indicated format.

D Notice that the Field Properties section does not contain a Field Size box. You cannot set the field size for date fields. The options on the Field Properties list change for each data type.

7. Now define another date field named **Last Visit**, as shown in the following illustration. Set the Format to Short Date, as shown at the bottom of the illustration.

Field Name	Data Type	Descri
Pet ID	Text	Primary key for Pet table
Pet Name	Text	
Pet Type	Text	
Breed	Text	
Gender	Text	
Color	Text	
Date of Birth	Date/Time	
▶ Last Visit	Date/Time	

Field Properties

General | Lookup

Format	Short Date
Input Mask	

Define Currency and Number Fields

In the next few steps, you will define two more fields. You will set the Data Type to Currency for one of the fields and Number for the other. Currency and number fields can be used in calculations. Furthermore, fields formatted with the Currency data type will display a dollar sign, a decimal point, and two decimal places whenever you enter data into the fields.

8. Define the Expenditures and Number of Visits fields as shown in the following illustration:

A Set the Data Types and enter the descriptions as shown. Leave the Field Properties at the bottom of the dialog box with the default settings. Number fields normally have a Field Size of Long Integer, as shown here. Keep in mind that choosing Field Properties can be an involved process that often requires extensive knowledge of Access. ──

Field Name	Data Type	Description
Pet ID	Text	Primary key for Pet table
Pet Name	Text	
Pet Type	Text	
Breed	Text	
Gender	Text	
Color	Text	
Date of Birth	Date/Time	
Last Visit	Date/Time	
Expenditures	Currency	Total expenditures on this pet from time of first visit
▶ Number of Visits	Number	Total number of visits for this pet

Field Properties

General | Lookup

Field Size	Long Integer
Format	

9. Now continue with the next topic, in which you will define a primary key for the table.

Working with Primary Keys

Most Access tables have one field defined as the primary key. The field chosen to be the primary key field must contain unique data; for example, numbers or codes. The Pet ID field will be the primary key in the Pets table. A unique Pet ID will identify each pet and no two pets can have the same ID. You can't designate a field like Name as the primary key because than one person can have the same name. In Table Design view, you specify a primary key by clicking in the desired field and clicking the Primary Key button on the Access toolbar. Access will also prompt you to choose a primary key field if you close a table that has not been assigned one. If you allow Access to choose your primary key for you, it will create a new field called ID, which will be defined as an AutoNumber so that each record will have unique data in that field. Most often this is not what we want from our databases, so it is best to choose your own primary key. Your tables will be automatically sorted on the field you designate as the primary key.

 Hands-On 1.4 **Choose a Primary Key**

In this exercise, you will choose a primary key for your database.

1. Follow these steps to choose a primary key:

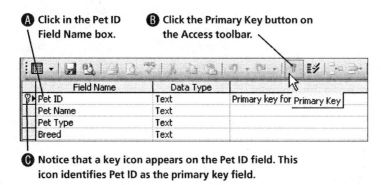

Ⓐ Click in the Pet ID Field Name box. Ⓑ Click the Primary Key button on the Access toolbar.

Ⓒ Notice that a key icon appears on the Pet ID field. This icon identifies Pet ID as the primary key field.

Saving Database Objects

An Access database is a container that holds tables and other types of objects. The entire database is saved as a single file onto a hard disk or diskette. However, you must also save the objects within the database. Database objects are assigned names when they are saved. This allows you to identify the objects at a later time. Like fields, a database object name can be up to 64 characters in length and may contain letters, numbers, spaces, and other types of characters.

FROM THE KEYBOARD
Ctrl+S to save open object

You save an open object by clicking the Save 🖫 button on the Access toolbar. Access will also prompt you to save an object if you attempt to close the object without saving the changes.

Hands-On 1.5 **Save the Table**

In this exercise, you will save the table to your database.

1. Click the Save button on the Access toolbar.

2. Type the name **Pets** in the Save As box and click OK.

3. Follow these steps to close the table:

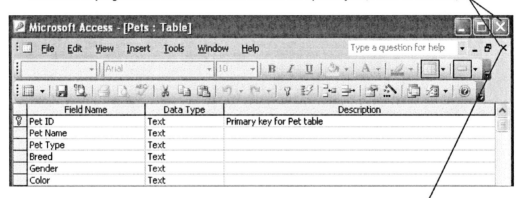

Ⓐ Notice that there are two Close buttons in the Access window. The top button closes the entire Access program and the bottom button closes the open object (a table in this case).

Ⓑ Click the bottom Close button and the table will close.

A Pets icon will appear in the Tables section of the Access window. You have completed the process of setting up a table! At this point, you could set up additional tables or other types of objects. Instead, in Hands-On 1.6, you will enter data into the Pets table. To accomplish this, you will use Datasheet view.

Opening Objects

The Database window provides access to all database objects. You can select any object by clicking the appropriate objects button then clicking the desired object. Once you select an object, you can open the object or display it in Design view.

FROM THE KEYBOARD

[Enter] to open selected object

[Ctrl]+[Enter] to open selected object in Design view

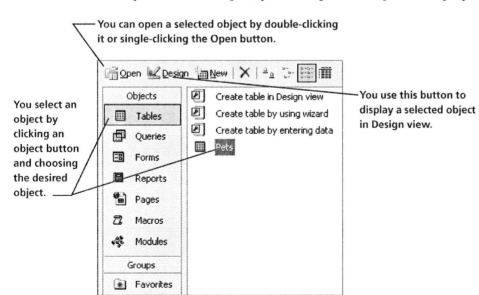

You can open a selected object by double-clicking it or single-clicking the Open button.

You use this button to display a selected object in Design view.

You select an object by clicking an object button and choosing the desired object.

Entering Data in Datasheet View

In Hands-On 1.3 you used Design view to set up the Pets table. Design view lets you set up or modify the structure of tables. However, to enter data into a table, you must display the table in Datasheet view. Remember, you can open a table in Datasheet view from the Access Database window. Once a table is opened in Datasheet view, you can enter data the same way it is entered into an Excel worksheet. The Tab key can be used to move forward one table cell and Shift+Tab can be used to move back one cell. You can also click in any cell and enter new data or edit existing data.

 Hands-On 1.6   Enter Data

In this exercise, you will enter data into the Pets table.

1. Follow these steps to open the Pets table in Datasheet view:

A Make sure the Tables button is chosen then click the Pets table icon.

B Click the Open button. You could also have opened the Pets table by double-clicking the Pets icon.

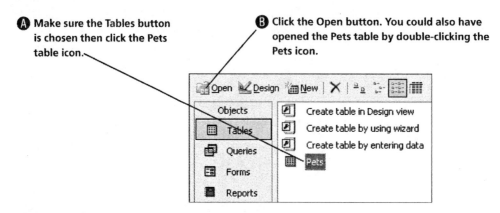

2. Follow these steps to explore the Datasheet view window:
   Keep in mind that your window may have different dimensions than shown here.

A Notice that many of the toolbar buttons are different from those in the Design view window.

B Notice that the field names are displayed as column headings.

C Data are entered into the rows (although you only see one row at this point). Each row is a record. For example, each row will contain all of the data for one pet. You use the Tab key to move from one field to the next within a row (or you can click in the desired row or field).

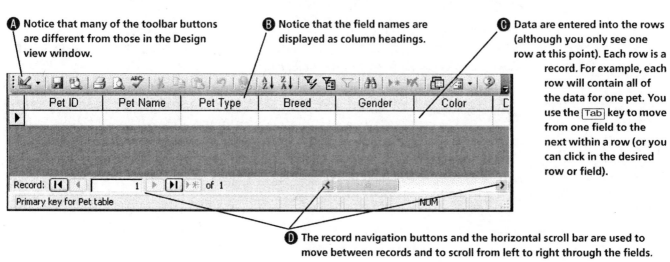

D The record navigation buttons and the horizontal scroll bar are used to move between records and to scroll from left to right through the fields.

3. Follow these steps to begin entering a record:

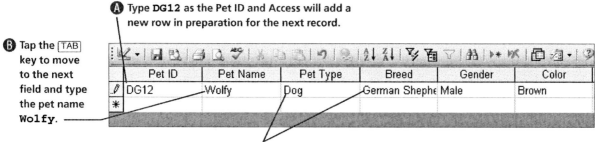

Ⓐ Type **DG12** as the Pet ID and Access will add a new row in preparation for the next record.

Ⓑ Tap the TAB key to move to the next field and type the pet name **Wolfy**.

Ⓒ Continue entering the data shown here using the TAB key to move between fields. When you get to the Breed field, type the phrase **German Shepherd**. Because the phrase is wider than the column Access scrolls the column so you can enter the text.

4. If necessary, use the horizontal scroll bar to scroll to the right until the fields shown here are visible.

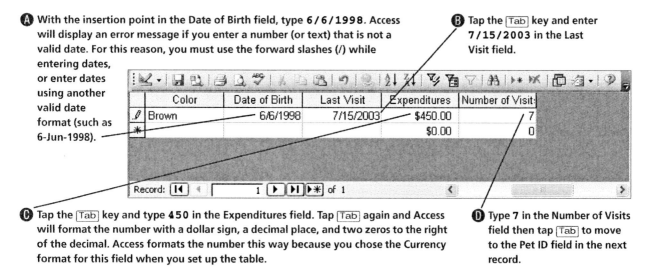

5. Follow these steps to enter data in the remaining fields:

Ⓐ With the insertion point in the Date of Birth field, type **6/6/1998**. Access will display an error message if you enter a number (or text) that is not a valid date. For this reason, you must use the forward slashes (/) while entering dates, or enter dates using another valid date format (such as 6-Jun-1998).

Ⓑ Tap the Tab key and enter **7/15/2003** in the Last Visit field.

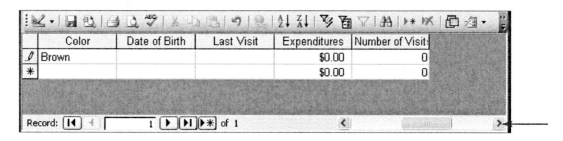

Ⓒ Tap the Tab key and type **450** in the Expenditures field. Tap Tab again and Access will format the number with a dollar sign, a decimal place, and two zeros to the right of the decimal. Access formats the number this way because you chose the Currency format for this field when you set up the table.

Ⓓ Type **7** in the Number of Visits field then tap Tab to move to the Pet ID field in the next record.

Notice that Access right-aligns the dates and numbers in the last four fields. Access always right-aligns entries that can be used in calculations.

6. Use these guidelines to enter the following records into the table:

- Use the [Tab] key to move between fields.
- Make sure to use forward slashes (/) when entering the dates.
- Do not type dollar signs when entering numbers in the Expenditures field. However, do type a decimal point followed by the indicated decimals.
- Do not try to stack the words under Breed or Color as they appear here. For example, "White with patches" should appear on the same line in your datasheet.

Pet ID	Pet Name	Pet Type	Breed	Gender	Color	Date of Birth	Last Visit	Expenditures	Number of Visits
DG13	Dillon	Dog	Mutt	Male	Black	10/5/2001	7/7/2003	150.55	3
CT89	Puffy	Cat	Siamese	Female	White with patches	12/12/2000	7/7/2003	30.00	1
RB23	Bugs	Rabbit	Jack	Unknown	Brown	6/7/1999	9/7/2003	600.50	4
CT02	Max	Cat	Unknown	Male	White	1/7/1996	9/7/2003	1450.55	20
CT16	Stripes	Cat	Tortoise shell	Male	Black and brown	10/8/2000	7/15/2003	450.00	9
DG14	Fetch	Dog	German Sheperd	Male	Black and brown	8/12/1999	9/10/2003	345.00	3

7. Check your data carefully to make sure it is error free. Accuracy is extremely important when entering data.

8. When you have finished checking your work, choose File→Close from the menu bar. *Access will close the table and the Database window will be displayed. You can close objects with either the File→Close command or by clicking the Close button (as you did earlier). Notice that Access did not prompt you to save the table. Access automatically saves data entered into a table. In fact, it saves the data one record at a time as you enter it.*

Printing Tables

It is very important that you enter data accurately. There are few things more upsetting to customers and other business contacts than seeing their names misspelled and careless data entry errors. For this reason, you should check your data for accuracy after it has been entered. Perhaps the best way to check data accuracy is to print the contents of your tables. Proof-reading hard copy (paper printout) is usually the best way to spot errors.

FROM THE KEYBOARD
[Ctrl]+[P] to display Print dialog box

The Print 🖨 button on the Access toolbar sends the entire contents of a table open in Datasheet view to the current printer. You must display the Print dialog box if you want to change printers, adjust the number of copies to be printed, or set other printing options. You display the Print dialog box with the File→Print command. The following illustration highlights the most frequently used options available in the Print dialog box.

You choose printers from this drop-down list.

You specify the number of copies here. The Collate option is useful when you are printing more than one copy of a multi-page table. If the Collate box is checked, all pages of the first copy are printed before the second copy begins printing, etc.

You can choose to print all pages, a range of pages, or selected records.

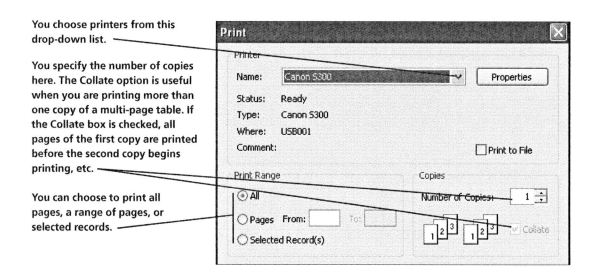

Working with Print Preview

The Print Preview button on the Access toolbar displays the Print Preview window. Print Preview lets you see exactly how a table will look when printed. Print Preview can save time, paper, and wear-and-tear on your printer. Print Preview is especially useful when printing a table with a large number of records. It is always wise to preview a large table before sending it to the printer. When you display the Print Preview window, the Access toolbar is replaced by the Print Preview toolbar.

Hands-On 1.7   Use Print Preview

In this exercise, you will see how your table would look if printed.

1. Click the Pets 🏢 Pets button in the Access window then click the 🗁 Open button on the Database toolbar. The Database toolbar is located just above the Objects bar.
   The Pets table will open in Datasheet view.

2. Click the Print Preview 🔍 button on the Access toolbar.

3. Zoom in by clicking anywhere on the table.

4. Zoom out by clicking anywhere on the table.
   Notice that only six of the table's columns are visible in the Print Preview window. It is a good thing that you used Print Preview before printing the table! You should hold off on printing the table until you change the page orientation and margins.

5. Click the Close button on the Print Preview toolbar to exit without printing.

Adjusting Column Widths

You may need to adjust table column widths so you can see the entire contents of table cells on a printout. In Datasheet view, you can use several techniques to adjust column widths, as described in the following Quick Reference table.

QUICK REFERENCE: ADJUSTING COLUMN WIDTHS

Adjustment Technique	Procedure
AutoFit a column to fit the widest entry in the column	Double-click the border between two column headings or choose Format→Column Width and click Best Fit.
Set a precise column width	Choose Format→Column Width and enter the desired width.
Set column widths to the default standard width	Choose Format→Column Width, check the Standard Width box, and click OK.

 Hands-On 1.8   **Adjust Column Widths**

In this exercise, you will adjust the column widths in the table so you can see the full contents of the cells.

1. Follow these steps to manually adjust the width of the Pet ID column:

Ⓐ Position the mouse pointer on the border between the Pet ID and Pet Name column headings. Notice that the Adjust pointer appears.

Ⓑ Drag the border to the left until the Pet ID column is just wide enough to display the column heading (Pet ID).

Pet ID	Pet Name	Pet Type
CT02	Max	Cat
CT16	Stripes	Cat
CT89	Puffy	Cat

2. Position the mouse pointer on the border between the Pet Name and Pet Type columns. Double-click when the adjust pointer appears.
This technique can be tricky so keep trying until the Pet Name column shrinks to the width of the heading. If the column has entries wider than the heading, the width will adjust to fit the widest entry in the column.

Pet ID	Pet Name	Pet Type
CT02	Max	Cat
CT16	Stripes	Cat
CT89	Puffy	Cat

3. Follow these steps to AutoFit the width of all columns:

Ⓐ Position the mouse pointer on the Pet ID column heading then press and hold the left mouse button. The column selection pointer will appear, as shown here.

Ⓑ Drag the mouse over all 11 column headings in the table to select them.

Ⓒ Choose Format→Column Width from the menu bar and click the Best Fit button.

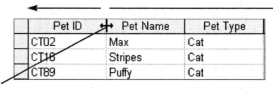

Pet ID	Pet Name	Pet Type
CT02	Max	Cat
CT16	Stripes	Cat
CT89	Puffy	Cat

4. Click anywhere in the table to deselect the columns.

5. Scroll to the left and notice that all column widths fit the widest entry (or heading) in the columns.

Working with Margins and Page Orientation

Many tables are quite wide and may not fit on a single printed page. Fortunately, most printers can print text both vertically in Portrait orientation and horizontally in Landscape orientation. Landscape orientation may allow a wide table (such as the Pets table) to print on a single page. You can set the orientation of a page by issuing the File→Page Setup command, clicking the Page tab, and choosing the desired orientation. The margins can also be adjusted in the Page Setup dialog box.

 Hands-On 1.9   **Set Page Orientation and Margins, and Print**

In this exercise, you will adjust the page orientation and margins of the table. Then you will print the table.

1. Choose File→Page Setup from the Access menu bar.

2. On the Margins tab, set all four margins to **0.25** (that's 0.25 not 25).

3. Click the Page tab and choose the Landscape option.

4. Click OK to complete the changes.

5. Click the Print Preview 🔍 button on the Access toolbar.

6. If necessary, zoom in by clicking anywhere on the table. Scroll left or right to view all columns in the table.
   Notice that the page orientation is now horizontal (Landscape). All columns should be visible on the page.

7. Print the table by clicking the Print 🖨 button on the Print Preview toolbar.

8. Click the Close button on the Print Preview toolbar when you have finished.

9. Now close the table by choosing File→Close from the Access menu bar.

10. Click the Yes button when Access asks if you want to save the changes.

11. Close Access by choosing File→Exit from the Access menu bar.

12. Now continue with the end-of-lesson questions and exercises.

 Concepts Review

True/False Questions

1.	An Access database can have a maximum of one table.	TRUE	FALSE
2.	Datasheet view is used to set up the structure of tables.	TRUE	FALSE
3.	You cannot modify the size of a field in Design view.	TRUE	FALSE
4.	A database is like a container because it can hold several types of objects, including tables.	TRUE	FALSE
5.	The Format→Column Width command can be used to set precise column widths.	TRUE	FALSE
6.	The page orientation can be changed with the File→Print command.	TRUE	FALSE
7.	Portrait orientation causes a table to print horizontally on a page.	TRUE	FALSE
8.	Tables are composed of records.	TRUE	FALSE
9.	Text, Number, and Currency are examples of data types.	TRUE	FALSE
10.	You can enter data into a table in Design view.	TRUE	FALSE

Multiple Choice Questions

1. What is the maximum number of characters that a field name may contain?

   a. 8

   b. 32

   c. 64

   d. 255

2. Which of the following are examples of data types?

   a. Text

   b. Number

   c. Currency

   d. All of the above

3. Which of the following commands is used to change the page orientation?

   a. File→Print

   b. File→Page Setup

   c. Format→Page Orientation

   d. Format→Print Preview

4. What happens when you double-click the border between two column headings in Datasheet view?

   a. The table is closed

   b. The column width is set to the default column width

   c. A new column is inserted

   d. The column width is AutoFit to the widest entry

Skill Builders

Set Up a Table in Design View

In this exercise, you will set up a new database for the Tropical Getaways travel company. Tropical Getaways is an exciting new travel company that specializes in inexpensive vacations to tropical locations worldwide. You have been asked to set up a database to track clients and trips. You will begin by creating the first table for the database.

1. Start Access, choose Create a New File, and then choose Blank Database from the Task Pane.

2. Assign the name **Tropical Getaways** to your new database and save it to your file storage location.
   The Tables object list should be displayed in the Access Database window.

3. Double-click the Create Table in Design View option to begin setting up a new table in Design view.

4. Type **Customer ID** as the first field name and tap the Tab key.

5. Click the drop-down ▾ button in the Data Type box and choose AutoNumber.
   Access will automatically assign sequential Customer IDs when you enter data in this table.

6. Click the Primary Key 🔑 button on the toolbar to make Customer ID the primary key.

7. Set up the remainder of this table using the field names, data types, and options shown in the following table. Keep in mind that you have already set up the Customer ID field.

Field Name	Data Type	Field Size	Primary Key	Description
Customer ID	AutoNumber	Long Integer	Yes	
Firstname	Text	30		
Lastname	Text	30		
Address	Text	50		
City	Text	30		
State	Text	2		
Zip	Text	9		
Profile	Text	20		The profile indicates the category of trips the customer prefers

8. When you have finished, click the Datasheet 🔲 view button on the left end of the Access toolbar.
   The veiw button can be used to switch between various views.

9. Click Yes when Access asks if you wish to save the table.

10. Type **Customers** as the table name, click OK, and enter the following four records. The Customer ID numbers should be entered automatically because Customer ID has an AutoNumber data type. Customer ID will be entered automatically after you type the data into the FirstName field.

Customer ID	Firstname	Lastname	Address	City	State	Zip	Profile
1	Debbie	Thomas	450 Crestwood Lane	Austin	TX	78752	Adventure
2	Wilma	Boyd	855 State Street	Richmond	NY	12954	Leisure
3	Ted	Wilkins	900 C Street	Fort Worth	TX	76104	Adventure
4	Alice	Simpson	2450 Ridge Road	Fort Worth	TX	76105	Family

11. When you have finished, choose File→Close from the Access menu bar to close the table. *Access automatically saves the data you entered. You will set up another table in the next Skill Builder exercise.*

Skill Builder 1.2   Set Up a Table in Design View

In this exercise, you will set up another table for the Tropical Getaways database.

1. Double-click the Create Table in Design View option to begin setting up a new table in Design view.

2. Set up the table using the following structure:

Field Name	Data Type	Field Size/Format	Primary Key	Description
Trip ID	Text	8	Yes	Four- to eight-character unique identifier for each trip
Customer ID	Number	Long Integer		ID number from Customers table
Destination	Text	50		
Category	Text	30		All trips have a category such as Adventure, Leisure, etc.
Departure Date	Date/Time	Short Date		
Return Date	Date/Time	Short Date		
Cost	Currency			

3. Close and save the table as **Trips**.

4. Double-click the icon for the Trips table in the Access database window and enter the following data. Do not type the dollar signs and commas when entering the Cost numbers. Access will add these for you because you chose the Auto Number data type when you set up the Cost field.

Trip ID	Customer ID	Destination	Category	Departure Date	Return Date	Cost
Adv01	1	Kenyan Safari	Adventure	8/5/04	9/4/04	$6,600
Lei01	2	Caribbean Cruise	Leisure	9/19/04	9/28/04	$2,390
Adv02	1	Amazon Jungle Trek	Adventure	8/7/04	9/14/04	$7,765
Fam01	4	Orlando	Family	3/4/04	3/10/04	$3,400

5. Close the Trips table when you have finished.
The Tables objects list should now display both the Customers and Trips table icons.

Skill Builder 1.3   Print the Table

In this exercise, you will print the Customers table. The Tropical Getaways database should be open, and the Customers and Trips tables should be visible in the Access Database window.

1. Double-click the Customers table to open it in Datasheet view.
   You can always open a table in Datasheet view by double-clicking it.

2. Adjust the widths of all columns to display the widest entries in the columns.

3. Use the Print Preview ⬚ button to preview the table.

4. Zoom in on the table by clicking anywhere on it.

5. Feel free to print the table and check your data for accuracy.

6. Close Print Preview when you have finished.

7. Close the table and choose Yes when Access asks if you want to save the changes.

8. Now open the Trips table and adjust the column widths to fit the widest entries in the columns.
   Notice that the records in the Trips table are now sorted by Trip ID since that is the primary key.

9. Print the table and check your data for accuracy.

10. Close the table and save the changes when you have finished.

11. Exit from Access by choosing File→Exit from the menu bar.

Skill Builder 1.4   **Use the Database Wizard**

In this exercise, you will use the Database Wizard to set up a database.

1. Start Access and the task pane will appear. If the task pane is not displayed, use the View→Task Pane command to display it.

2. Choose the Create a New File option in the task pane.

3. Under Templates, choose the On My Computer option.

4. Click the Databases tab in the Templates box to view the available predefined databases. *The Database Wizard is initiated when you choose any of these predefined databases.*

5. Double-click the Contact Management database and save it to your file storage location as **Contact Management Database**.

6. Click Next to bypass the first wizard screen. *The second wizard screen displays the predefined tables in the Contact Management database and the fields in each table. You remove fields by unchecking them or add additional fields by scrolling through the field list and checking the desired additional fields (shown in italics).*

7. Click Next to bypass the screen and accept the default fields.

8. Continue to click the Next button on the next few screens. You will be offered various forms and report formats; feel free to choose any options you desire.

9. Click the Finish button when you have finished choosing options. *The wizard will create the database.*

10. Feel free to use your new database. You will be exposed to features that you have not learned about yet, and will certainly be impressed with the database the wizard has created. *At this point, you could add tables, fields, and other objects to your database or modify the objects already in the database.*

11. When you have finished examining your database, close it, and exit from Access.

 **Assessments**

Assessment 1.1   **Create a Table**

In this exercise, you will begin creating a database for Classic Cars. Classic Cars is an organization devoted to tracking, categorizing, and preserving classic automobiles. You will begin by creating tables to track collectors and cars.

1. Start Access and create a new database named **Classic Cars**.

2. Create a new table with the following structure:

Field Name	Data Type	Field Size	Primary Key	Description
Collector ID	AutoNumber	Long Integer	Yes	
Firstname	Text	30		
Lastname	Text	30		
Address	Text	50		
City	Text	30		
State	Text	2		
Zip	Text	9		
Era of Interest	Text	20		This field identifies the time period that the collector is most interested in
Collection Size	Number	Long Integer		Number of cars in collection

3. Click the Datasheet ▦ view button and save the table with the name **Collectors**.

4. Enter the following records into the table:

Collector ID	Firstname	Lastname	Address	City	State	Zip	Era of Interest	Collection size
1	Cindy	Johnson	4220 Edward Street	Northlake	IL	60164	1950s	42
2	Tammy	Olson	1200 Big Pine Drive	Moses Lake	WA	98837	1960s	6
3	Ed	Larkson	2300 Watson Street	Cainesville	OH	43701	Early 1900s	34
4	Bob	Barker	6340 Palm Drive	Rockridge	FL	32955	1950s	7

5. AutoFit the width of all columns to fit the largest entry/heading in the columns.

6. Use Print Preview to preview the table. If necessary, switch the orientation to Landscape and reduce the margins until the table fits on one page.

7. Print the table.

8. Close the table when you have finished and save any changes.

9. Create another new table with the following structure:

Field Name	Data Type	Field Size/Format	Primary Key	Description
Car ID	Text	15	Yes	Up to 15 characters to uniquely identify each car
Collector ID	Number	Long Integer		ID number from Collectors table
Year	Text	20		
Make	Text	30		
Model	Text	50		
Color	Text	30		
Condition	Text	30		
Value	Currency			Estimated value

10. Click the Datasheet ▦ view button and save the table with the name **Cars**.

11. Enter the following records into the table:

Car ID	CollectorID	Year	Make	Model	Color	Condition	Value
CJ01	1	58	Chevrolet	Corvette	Red and white	Mint	$65,000
TO05	2	62	Chevrolet	Corvette	Blue	Excellent	$30,000
CJ22	1	59	Ford	Thunderbird	Tan	Good	$20,000
BB03	4	58	Chevrolet	Corvette	Black	Excellent	$35,000

12. AutoFit the width of all columns to fit the largest entry/heading in the columns.

13. Use Print Preview to preview the table.

14. Print the table.

15. Close the table when you have finished and save any changes.

16. Exit from Access when you have finished.

Critical Thinking

Create Tables

Linda Holmes is a real estate agent specializing in investment properties. She needs database software to help her manage her business. She has reviewed commercially available software but has found it inadequate for her needs. Instead, Linda has hired you to create a customized Access database.

Create a new, blank database for Linda named **Holmestead Realty**. The first two categories of information Linda wants to track are contact information for sellers and listing information for the properties they wish to sell. Follow these guidelines to set up two tables in your new database:

- Name the first table **Contacts** and the second table **Listings**.
- Use the field names, data types, and field properties listed in the following table.
- Leave all other field properties set to their default values.

Contacts Table

Field Name	Data Type	Field Properties
Seller ID	Auto Number	Primary key
FirstName	Text	
LastName	Text	
SpouseName	Text	Field size 30
Address	Text	
City	Text	
State	Text	
Zip	Text	
Phone	Text	
Contact Type	Text	

Listings Table

Field Name	Data Type	Field Properties
MLS#	Number	Primary key
Street#	Number	
Address	Text	
Price	Currency	
Listing Date	Date	Short Date format
Expiration Date	Date	Short Date format
Commission Rate	Number	Field Size: Decimal, Format: Percent, Precision: 18, Scale: 3, Decimal Places: 1
Seller ID	Number	

Enter the following data into your completed tables. Be sure to check the data carefully when finished. Adjust all column widths to fit the widest entry in each column. Print copies of both tables when you have finished.

Contacts

Seller ID	FirstName	LastName	Spouse Name	Address	City	ST	Zip	Phone	Contact Type
1	John	Desmond	Lydia	1020 Brevard Road	Asheville	NC	28801	(828) 298-5698	Investor
2	David	Armstrong		15 Dover Street	Swannanoa	NC	28778	(828) 669-8579	Investor
3	Sharon	Carter		9 Forest Pine Circle	Asheville	NC	28803	(828) 277-3658	Investor
4	Jeff	Jones	Susan	107 Glen Meadows Place	Arden	NC	28704	(828) 687-5786	Investor
5	Jamie	Stevens		10 Knollwood Drive	Asheville	NC	28804	(828) 274-6643	Investor
6	Phil	Wallace	Jennifer	1571 Brannon Road	Asheville	NC	28801	(828) 252-2365	Investor

Listings

MLS #	Street #	Address	Price	Listing Date	Expiration Date	Commission Rate	Seller ID
52236	1132	Richwood Road	$55,000	1/14/04	7/14/04	6.0%	4
52358	14	Dover Street	$70,000	5/30/03	11/30/03	7.0%	2
52369	6	Thoroughbred Lane	$125,000	9/25/03	3/25/04	6.0%	1
52425	218	Wildflower Road	$329,500	6/2/03	12/2/03	4.5%	2
52511	403	Hawks Landing	$150,000	9/23/03	3/23/04	6.0%	3
52524	64	Hastings Street	$112,000	4/6/04	10/6/04	4.5%	6
52526	137	Woodbridge Lane	$80,000	3/21/04	9/21/04	4.5%	6
52649	23	Edwards Avenue	$70,000	7/15/03	1/15/04	6.0%	5
52650	24	Edwards Avenue	$75,000	7/15/03	1/15/04	6.0%	5

LESSON 2

Modifying and Maintaining Tables

In this lesson, you will make changes to the tables in the Pinnacle Pet Care database. You will learn how to change the structure of tables and edit records within a database. You will create a table using the Table Wizard and set up validation rules to ensure that users enter valid data.

IN THIS LESSON

Microsoft Office Access 2003 objectives covered in this lesson

Objective Number	Skill Sets and Skills	Concept Page References	Exercise Page References
AC03S-1-2	Create and modify tables	34, 41	34–36, 42–44
AC03S-1-3	Define and modify field types	50	50–52
AC03S-1-4	Modify field properties	44–45	45–47
AC03S-2-2	Find and move among records	36–37	37–39
AC03S-3-6	Filter records	40	40–41

Additional learning resources are available at labpub.com/learn/access03/

Case Study

Sometimes after the initial tables in Access have been created, it's necessary to make changes to them. It is also important to ensure that the minimum of errors occur when people enter data into the tables. Penny Johnson has created two of the tables for the database and will now go through modifying them, using validation rules and input masks to minimize entry error. Penny has also talked with some of the employees and has decided to add additional tables and modify the existing tables to hold more information that will be needed by Pinnacle Pet Care. She would also like to show employees how to find certain records and to sort through the data using filters.

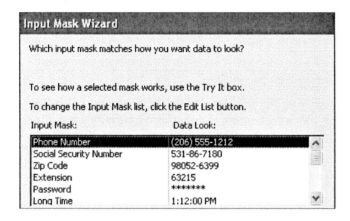

Penny uses the Input Mask Wizard to set up the phone number.

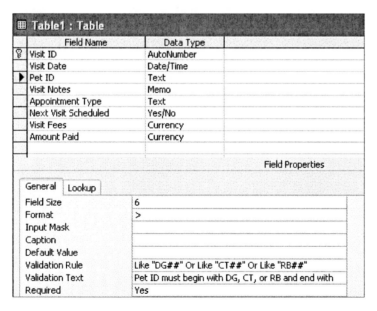

Many data entry errors can be eliminated by using Validation Rules in the Table Design.

Changing the Structure of a Table

You can change the structure of a table after it has been created. For example, you may need to change the size or name of a field, or add a new field. Structural changes are made to a table in Design view.

How Changing the Structure Can Impact Data

You must be careful when changing the structure of a table, especially if data has already been entered. For example, imagine that a field has a length of 30 and you have already entered records into the table. If you reduce the field length to 20, you may delete up to 10 characters from some records. Access will usually provide a warning message if you attempt to make a change that has the potential of destroying data in a field.

Switching between Object Views

The Datasheet view button appears on the left end of the Access toolbar whenever you are in Design view. You can switch from Design view to Datasheet view by clicking the Datasheet view button.

Likewise, the Design view button appears on the left end of the Access toolbar when you are in Datasheet view. You can switch to Design view by clicking the Design view button.

Setting the Default Value of Fields

Access lets you set default values for fields. The default value is automatically entered in new records when you enter data in Datasheet view. This can be convenient if a field is typically set to a certain value. For example, you will set the default value of the Number of Visits field to 1. Pets will be entered into the database when they make their first visit to the clinic. By setting the Number of Visits field to 1, you can skip the Number of Visits field when entering data for a new pet. In Design view, default values are set in the Field Properties area at the bottom of the dialog box.

⚠TIP! *Only set a default value if the field will have that value the majority of the time.*

 Hands-On 2.1 **Change the Table Structure**

In this exercise, you will open the Pinnacle Pet Care database you created in Lesson 1, Creating Tables and Entering Data and change the structure of the table.

Change a Field's Properties

1. Start Access and open the Pinnacle Pet Care database.
2. Click the icon in the Access window then click the Design button on the Database toolbar.
   The Pets table will open in Design view.

3. Follow these steps to change the default value for the Number of Visits field:

Field Name	Data Type	
Pet ID	Text	Primary key for Pet table
Pet Name	Text	
Pet Type	Text	
Breed	Text	
Gender	Text	
Color	Text	
Date of Birth	Date/Time	
Last Visit	Date/Time	
Expenditures	Currency	Total expenditures on thi
▶ Number of Visits	Number	Total number of visits for

A Click anywhere in the Number of Visits row (you may need to scroll down).

General | Lookup

Field Size	Long Integer
Format	
Decimal Places	Auto
Input Mask	
Caption	
Default Value	1
Validation Rule	

B Change the Default Value to **1**.

Add a Field

In the next few steps, you will add a Customer ID field to the table. The Customer ID field will eventually link the Pets table to the Customers table.

4. Follow these steps to add the Customer ID field:

Field Name	Data Type	
Pet ID	Text	Primary key for Pet
Pet Name	Text	
Pet Type	Text	
Breed	Text	
Gender	Text	
Color	Text	
Date of Birth	Date/Time	
Last Visit	Date/Time	
Expenditures	Currency	Total expenditures c
Number of Visits	Number	Total number of visit
▶ Customer ID	Number	

General | Lookup

Field Size	Long Integer
Format	
Decimal Places	Auto

A Click in the box below Number of Visits and type **Customer ID**. Make sure to include a space between the words.

B Set the Data Type to Number.

C Take a moment to proof every field name. Make sure the spelling is correct and matches the spelling of the field names in this illustration. It is important that the field names be spelled correctly because they will be used in other objects throughout this course.

Switch Views and Add Customer IDs

5. Click the Datasheet ▦ view button on the left end of the Access toolbar and click Yes when Access asks if you want to save the table.
Notice that the order of the records has changed in the table. The records should now be sorted in alphabetical order based on the primary key field. The records were sorted when you closed the table and then reopened it. One of the benefits of choosing a primary key field (such as Pet ID) is that Access will sort the records based on the primary key field.

6. Now add the following Customer IDs into the table. Make sure you enter the correct Customer ID in each record. You may need to scroll to the left and right in the table to ensure that the correct Customer ID has been entered for each Pet ID. As you can see from this example, it can be difficult to add data to records after changing the structure of a table. For this reason, you should spend as much time as necessary designing and planning a database to minimize the number of changes required.

Make sure each Pet ID has the correct Customer ID.

Pet ID	Pet Name	Pet Type	Breed	Gender		Date of Birth	Last Visit	Expenditures	Number of Visits	Customer ID
CT02	Max	Cat	Unknown	Male	V	1/7/1996	9/7/2003	$1,450.55	20	2
CT16	Stripes	Cat	Tortoise shell	Female	Bla	8/2000	7/15/2003	$450.00	9	3
CT89	Puffy	Cat	Siamese	Female	W	2/2000	7/7/2003	$30.00	1	1
DG12	Wolfy	Dog	German Shepherd	Male		6/6/1998	7/15/2003	$450.00	7	3
DG13	Dillon	Dog	Mutt	Male		10/5/2001	7/7/2003	$150.55	3	1
DG14	Fetch	Dog	German Shepherd	Male		8/12/1999	9/10/2003	$345.00	3	3
RB23	Bugs	Rabbit	Jack	Unknown	B	6/7/1999	9/7/2003	$600.50	4	2

7. Leave the table in Datasheet view and continue with the next topic.
You will add a record and make other changes in Hands-On 2.2.

Understanding Record Management

In Datasheet view, the Access toolbar has several buttons that let you manage records. The following table defines four of these buttons.

RECORD MANAGEMENT BUTTONS

Button	Function
🔍 Find	Lets you locate a record by searching for a word or phrase (Replace lets you replace a word or phrase with another word or phrase)
▶* New Record	Adds a new record at the end of the table
▶✕ Delete Record	Deletes the current record
🖌 Filter by Selection	Lets you retrieve only records that contain the selected value

Navigating within a Table

In Datasheet view, a record navigation bar appears at the bottom of the Access program window. The following illustration defines the buttons on the navigation bar.

Go to the first record in the table.　Move forward one record.

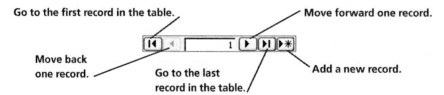

Move back one record.　Go to the last record in the table.　Add a new record.

Notice that the Back One Record button is "grayed out" in this illustration. This is because the insertion point is in the first record, as shown in the center of the navigation bar. In other words, there is no record to move back to.

 Hands-On 2.2 Manage Records

In this exercise, you will add data to the new record and navigate around the table. The Pets table should be in Datasheet view from the previous exercise.

Add a Record

1. Click the New Record ▶ button on the Access toolbar.
   The insertion point will move to a new record at the bottom of the table.

2. Enter the following data into the new record:

Pet ID	Pet Name	Pet Type	Breed	Pet Gender	Color	Date of Birth
CT92	Tony	Cat	Unknown	Male	Brown with black stripes	4/3/99

Last Visit	Expenditures	Number of Visits	Customer ID
7/7/2003	145	6	1

Navigate to Records

3. Follow these steps to navigate to various records:

A Notice the Pencil icon. It indicates that the current record is being edited.

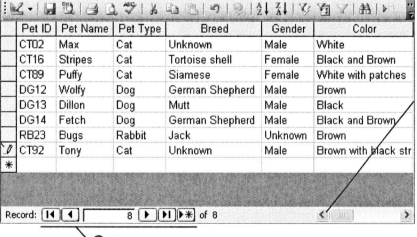

B If necessary, scroll to the left until the Pet ID field is visible.

C Click the various navigation buttons to browse through the records. The navigation buttons are useful when you have a large database with many records.

Delete a Record

4. Follow these steps to delete a record:

Ⓐ Click the record selector (square box) to the left of the CT89 record to select the entire record. The vertical column of boxes to the left of the records is called the Selection bar.

Ⓑ Click the Delete Record button on the Access toolbar.

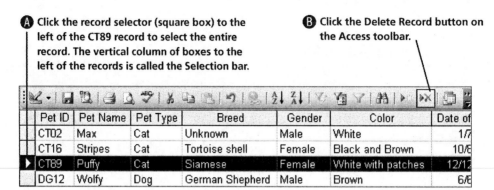

Pet ID	Pet Name	Pet Type	Breed	Gender	Color	Date of
CT02	Max	Cat	Unknown	Male	White	1/7
CT16	Stripes	Cat	Tortoise shell	Female	Black and Brown	10/8
CT89	Puffy	Cat	Siamese	Female	White with patches	12/12
DG12	Wolfy	Dog	German Shepherd	Male	Brown	6/8

Ⓒ Click the Yes button on the warning box that appears to confirm the deletion.

In the preceding steps, you selected the CT89 record prior to deleting it. You could actually have deleted the record by clicking anywhere in the CT89 row and clicking the Delete Record button. The Selection bar is most useful when you want to delete several records. You can select several records by dragging the mouse down the Selection bar.

Find Records

5. Click on any Pet ID in the Pet ID column.
In the following steps, you will search for Pet IDs. You must position the insertion point somewhere in the column that you wish to search prior to initiating the search.

6. Click the Find 🔍 button on the Access toolbar.

7. Follow these steps to conduct the search:

Ⓐ Type **ct92** in the Find What box.

Find and Replace

Find	Replace

Find What: ct92

Look In: Pet ID ▾

Match: Whole Field ▾

Search: All ▾

☐ Match Case ☑ Search Fields As Formatted

Ⓑ Notice that the Look In field indicates that you are searching for a Pet ID. In a large database, narrowing the search to a particular field can speed up the search.

Ⓒ Notice the Match Case box. It should be unchecked for the current search as shown here. This is because you typed the search string in lowercase (ct92) but the actual Pet ID in the database is in uppercase (CT92). Access will still find the Pet ID because the Match Case box is unchecked.

Ⓓ Click the Find Next button and the Pet ID CT92 will become selected.

8. Use the preceding steps to find Pet ID DG12.
   Keep in mind that the Find feature is most useful when you have a large database and the item you are searching for is not visible on the screen.

9. Click the Cancel button to close the dialog box.

Check Out the Replace Option

10. Click any record in the Gender column.

11. Click the Find 🔍 button on the Access toolbar.

12. Follow these steps to find and replace data:

Ⓐ Type **unknown** in the Find What box.   Ⓑ Click the Replace tab at the top of the dialog box.   Ⓒ Type **Male** in the Replace With box. Make sure you use a capital M; it will replace exactly like you type it here.

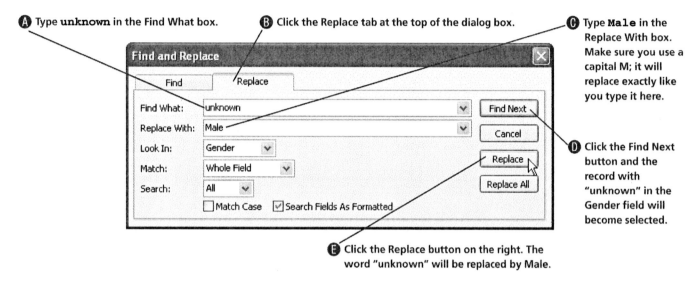

Ⓓ Click the Find Next button and the record with "unknown" in the Gender field will become selected.

Ⓔ Click the Replace button on the right. The word "unknown" will be replaced by Male.

13. Click the Cancel button to close the dialog box.

14. Leave the table open in Datasheet view and continue with the next topic.

Filtering Records in a Datasheet

Filters are used with datasheets and forms to let you temporarily view only those records that meet the criteria specified in the filter. The two most common types of filtering are filtering by selection and filtering by form. In both cases, the end result of applying a filter is that certain records are filtered out, leaving only those records that meet the filter criteria. The difference between the two filter types is the method that is used to apply the filter.

■ Filter by Selection ⛿—To filter by selection, you navigate to a record and click in a field that has the desired filter value. For example, if you are interested in seeing only records where the pet type is equal to dog, you should navigate to a record where the pet type is dog and click in the Pet Type field. When you click the Filter by Selection button, Access will only display records where the pet type is equal to dog.

■ Filter by Form ⛿—To filter by form, you first click the Filter by Form button and Access displays a form with blank fields. Then, type the desired filter value(s) into the blank field(s). You can also click in the blank fields and choose the desired values from drop-down lists. Access applies the filter when you click the Apply/Remove Filter button.

■ Apply Filter ▽—With this button you can apply filters. In addition, you can remove filters by clicking the Remove Filter button. Access then redisplays all records once a filter has been removed.

 Hands-On 2.3   Apply and Remove Filters

In this exercise, you will practice applying and removing filters.

Filter by Selection

1. Click in the Pet Type field on any record where the Pet Type is dog.

2. Click the Filter by Selection ⛿ button on the Access toolbar.
   Notice the navigation bar now indicates that you are viewing record 1 of 3 (Filtered).

3. Notice that only records with a Pet Type of dog are visible.

4. Click the Remove Filter ▽ button.
   The Navigation bar should once again indicate that seven records are available.

Add a Filter to a Filter

You can use the Filter by Selection button to filter records that have already been filtered.

5. Click in the Pet Type field on any record where the Pet Type is cat.

6. Click the Filter by Selection ⛿ button.

7. Notice that only three cat records are visible.

8. If necessary, click a record where "unknown" appears in the Breed field.

9. Click in the Breed field and click the Filter by Selection ⛿ button.
   Only two filtered records should now be available.

10. Click the Remove Filter ▽ button to remove the filtering.

Filter by Form

11. Click the Filter by Form 🔲 button.

12. Follow these steps to enter the desired criteria in the Filter by Form box:

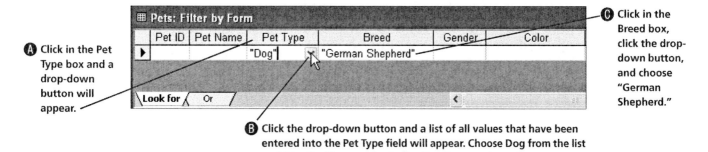

Ⓐ Click in the Pet Type box and a drop-down button will appear.

Ⓒ Click in the Breed box, click the drop-down button, and choose "German Shepherd."

Ⓑ Click the drop-down button and a list of all values that have been entered into the Pet Type field will appear. Choose Dog from the list and "Dog" will appear in the Pet Type box, as shown here.

13. Click the Apply Filter 🔽 button.

Browse through the filtered records and notice that they both have a Pet Type of "Dog" and Breed of "German Shepherd". Entering two values in the Filter by Form box has the same effect as applying a filter to a filter using the Filter by Selection tool.

14. Click the Remove Filter 🔽 button to remove the filter.

15. Feel free to experiment with filters. Remove all filtering when you have finished.

16. Close and Save the table when finished.

Using the Table Wizard

Access provides a Table Wizard to help you set up common tables. The Table Wizard provides a variety of sample tables and fields for each table. You can choose the sample fields to include in a table and the wizard will then build the table for you. In Hands-On 2.4, you will use the Table Wizard to set up a Customers table. Thus, you will have experience setting up tables in Design view and with the Table Wizard. In the future, you can use whichever method you prefer.

To start the Table Wizard, you click the 🔲 New button on the Access Database toolbar and choose Table Wizard from the New Table box. You can also double-click the Create Table by Using Wizard option that appears in the Tables section of the Access Database window.

Hands-On 2.4   Use the Table Wizard

In this exercise, you will use the Table Wizard to create a new table.

Use the Table Wizard to Create a New Table

1. Click the **New** button on the Access Database toolbar (located just above the Objects bar).

2. Choose Table Wizard and click OK.

3. Follow these steps to begin setting up a table:

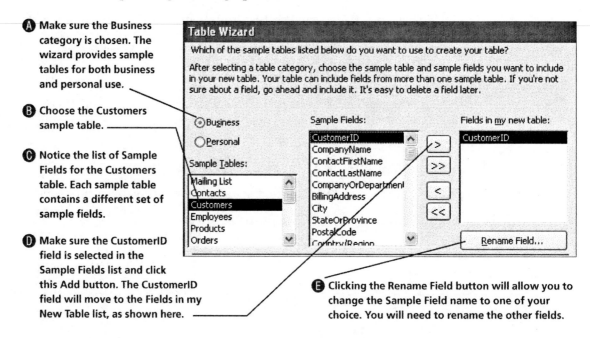

A Make sure the Business category is chosen. The wizard provides sample tables for both business and personal use.

B Choose the Customers sample table.

C Notice the list of Sample Fields for the Customers table. Each sample table contains a different set of sample fields.

D Make sure the CustomerID field is selected in the Sample Fields list and click this Add button. The CustomerID field will move to the Fields in my New Table list, as shown here.

E Clicking the Rename Field button will allow you to change the Sample Field name to one of your choice. You will need to rename the other fields.

4. Now add the ContactFirstName, ContactLastname, BillingAddress, City, StateOrProvince, PostalCode, and PhoneNumber fields by choosing them one at a time and clicking the Add button. Change the names of the fields as you add them, as shown in the following table.

TIP! *You can add a field by double-clicking it.*

Change this Field Name . . .	to this Name
ContactFirstName	FirstName
ContactLastName	LastName
BillingAddress	Address
City	*Leave as is*
StateOrProvince	State
PostalCode	Zip
PhoneNumber	Phone

5. Use the Remove Field ⟨<⟩ button if you mistakenly added a field and wish to remove it. Your completed Fields in My New Table list should match the example shown to the right (although your Phone field should be completely visible).

6. Click the Next button at the bottom of the dialog box.
   The next screen will propose the table name Customers and offer to set the primary key for you.

7. Leave the options set as they are by clicking the Next button.
   The next screen will ask you about relationships between tables.

8. Leave the option set to Not Related to Pets by clicking the Next button.
   The next screen will ask how you wish to display the completed table.

9. Choose the Modify the Table Design option and click the Finish button.
   Access will create the table for you and display it in Design view.

Modify the Table Structure

You may find Access wizards most useful for setting up tables and other objects. Once objects are set up, you can modify them to suit your particular needs. In the next few steps, you will use this approach by modifying the structure of the Customers table.

10. Follow these steps to explore the table you just created:

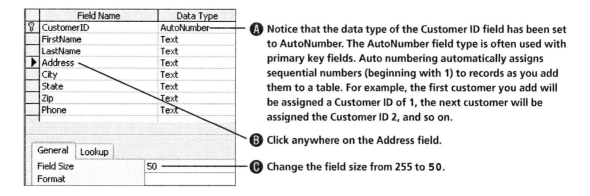

A Notice that the data type of the Customer ID field has been set to AutoNumber. The AutoNumber field type is often used with primary key fields. Auto numbering automatically assigns sequential numbers (beginning with 1) to records as you add them to a table. For example, the first customer you add will be assigned a Customer ID of 1, the next customer will be assigned the Customer ID 2, and so on.

B Click anywhere on the Address field.

C Change the field size from 255 to **50**.

11. Follow these steps to change the default value of the State field:

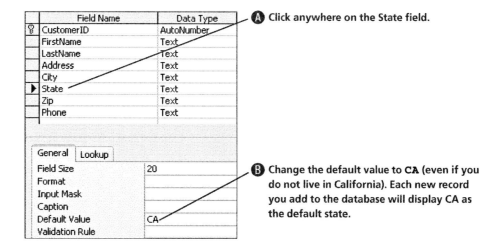

A Click anywhere on the State field.

B Change the default value to **CA** (even if you do not live in California). Each new record you add to the database will display CA as the default state.

Add New Fields

12. Follow these steps to insert a new date field:

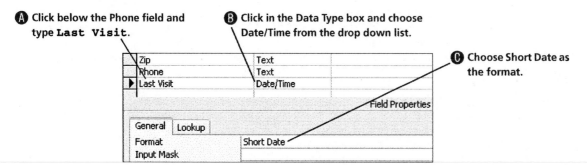

Ⓐ Click below the Phone field and type **Last Visit**.

Ⓑ Click in the Data Type box and choose Date/Time from the drop down list.

Ⓒ Choose Short Date as the format.

13. Now add a field named **Current Balance** and set the Data Type to Currency. Continue with the next topic, in which you will create an input mask for the phone field.

Working with Input Masks

Access lets you define input masks to help you enter formatted data. An input mask consists of a series of characters that define how the data is to be formatted. Input masks can be used for a variety of formatting tasks. For example, you can use an input mask to force all characters entered to be in uppercase or to automatically insert parenthesis and dashes in phone numbers. The input masks character string is entered in the Input Mask field property in Table Design view. Once an input mask is set up in a table, the mask formats display data in queries, forms, and reports.

The Input Mask Wizard

Setting up an input mask can be a tedious process. Fortunately, Access provides an Input Mask Wizard to help you set up common input mask formats. The following illustration discusses the process of setting up an input mask using the Input Mask Wizard.

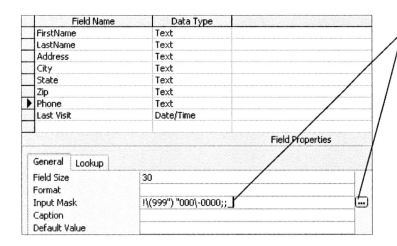

A Build button appears when you click in the Input Mask field property box. The Build button initiates the Input Mask Wizard. This input mask character string formats telephone numbers with parenthesis and dashes. The Input Mask Wizard can only be used with fields that have a Text or Date data type.

The Input Mask Wizard lets you choose common mask formats.

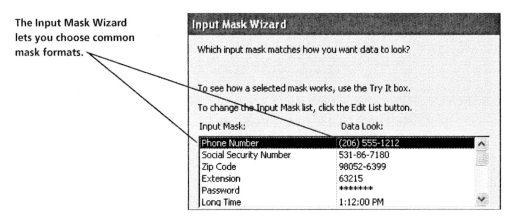

 Hands-On 2.5 **Use the Input Mask Wizard and Complete the Table**

In this exercise, you will set up two input masks and complete the table.

Set Up an Input Mask for the Phone Field

1. Click in the Phone field then click the Input Mask box in the Field Properties section of the window.

2. Click the Build ⊡ button on the right side of the Input Mask box and choose Yes to save the table.

3. Make sure the Phone Number mask is chosen in the first wizard screen and click Next.

4. Click Next on the second wizard screen to accept the proposed mask format.

5. Make sure the Without the Symbols option is chosen in the third screen and click Next.

6. Click the Finish button to complete the input mask.
   Access will display the input mask characters !(999) 000-0000;;_ in the Input Mask box.

Set Up an Input Mask for the Zip Field

7. Click in the Zip field then click in the Input Mask box.

8. Click the Build ⊡ button and choose Yes to save the table.

9. Choose the Zip Code mask and click the Finish button to accept the default options.
   You can click the Finish button at any time while using a wizard to accept the remaining default settings. Access will display the input mask characters 00000-9999;;_ in the Input Mask box.

Add Data to the Table

10. Click the Datasheet ▦ view button on the Access toolbar.

11. Click Yes when Access asks if you wish to save the table.
    Notice that the word AutoNumber is selected in the first empty record. This field is formatted with the AutoNumber data type so you will bypass it in the next step. Access will automatically assign the number 1 to the record when you begin entering data in the Firstname field.

12. Tap the [Tab] key to bypass the Customer ID field.

13. Type the name **Mark** in the Firstname field and the number 1 will appear in the Customer ID field.

14. Tap [Tab] and type **Roth** in the Lastname field.

15. Tap [Tab] and type **760 Maple Avenue** in the Address field.

16. Tap [Tab] and type **Fremont** in the City field.

17. Tap [Tab] and notice that the State field is set to CA.
    This is because you set CA as the default value for this field.

18. Tap [Tab] to bypass the State field (CA is correct) and type **94538** in the Zip field.
    You will notice that a hyphen appears to the right of the digits. This is because the Zip field has also been formatted with an input mask. The input mask inserts a hyphen between the first five and last four digits (if you use nine digits) of a zip code.

19. Tap [Tab] to bypass the last four digits of the zip code.

20. Type the area code **510** in the Phone field and the input mask will surround the number with parenthesis.

21. Complete the phone number by typing **2349090**.
    Access will format the number by inserting a hyphen between the 4 and the 9.

22. Tap [Tab] and type **7/7/03** in the Last Visit field.

23. Tap [Tab] and type **235** in the Current Balance field.

24. Now add the following two records to the table:
    The AutoNumber feature will insert numbers in the Customer ID field so just tap [Tab] when you reach that field. Also, do not type parenthesis in the phone numbers because the input mask will automatically apply them for you.

Customer ID	Firstname	Lastname	Address	City	State	Zip	Phone	Last Visit	Current Balance
2	Tony	Simpson	312 York Lane	Richmond	CA	94804	(510) 238-2233	9/7/03	185
3	Jason	Jones	2233 Crystal Street	San Mateo	CA	94403	(415) 312-2312	7/15/03	48

Print the Table

25. Adjust the width of all columns to fit the widest entry/heading in the columns. You can accomplish this by double-clicking the borders between the column headings. You can also select all of the columns by dragging the mouse pointer across the column headings and double-clicking the border between the column headings of any two selected columns. Finally, you can also select all columns and use the Format→Column Width command then click the Best Fit button.

26. Use the File→Page Setup command to set all four margins to **0.5**.

27. Notice that the Print Headings box is checked on the Margins tab.
In a moment, when you preview the table, you will notice a header and footer at the top and bottom of the page. The Print Headings box displays the header and footer. The Table Wizard turned on this option.

28. Set the orientation to Landscape using the Page tab in the Page Setup dialog box then click OK.

29. Use Print Preview to preview the table. Print the table if desired.

30. Close Print Preview and feel free to experiment with any of the topics you have learned so far in this lesson.

31. Save any changes to the table when you have finished experimenting then close it.

Creating Validation Rules

You have now set up and modified tables and entered, deleted, and filtered records. Nothing you have done so far will ensure that users enter valid data. Creating validation rules for data entry that the user must follow will do just that. Access will prevent data from being entered that does not follow these rules.

Understanding Validation Rules

- Specifying a specific range—You can set a specific range of values that are allowed in a field. For example the Visit Date would not be a valid date after today's date. (When you are entering a record of a customer's visit into the database, it would be for today's date or a date previous to today).

- Specifying a required field—A required field is one in which the user must enter data. This field cannot be left blank. The Pet ID is a field that should not be left blank.

- Specifying a default value—A default value is one that will appear in the field if the user does not enter anything in that field.

- Specifying a collection of legal values—A collection of legal values are the acceptable values to be entered into a specific field.

- Specifying format—To make data entry consistent, you can set the field so all text entered is displayed automatically in upper- or lowercase. Another example of a format is to set the number of characters necessary. If the Pet ID must be four characters, you can set it up so the user cannot enter any less than four characters.

- Validation text—Validation text is a message displayed when the user enters data that violates the rules set for that field.

Working with Wildcards

Wildcard characters are symbols that substitute for other characters when using the Find feature, in Queries, and in Table Design (validation rules). You use wildcards if you know only part of the value you are looking for or if you want to find values that begin with a specific letter or that match a certain pattern. For example, to find any word that begins with the letter B, you would type B*.

Three of the wildcard characters are the asterisk (*), which represents more than one character; the question mark (?), which represents only one character; and the pound symbol (#), which represents a single numeric value. In Hands-On 2.6, you will use wildcards because we want to identify values that begin with certain characters. You will set the validation rule for Pet ID, specify a collection of legal values, and set one value to DG##. This indicates that the value must begin with DG but can have any two numeric values after it. Using the wildcard characters allows you to access a number of values without having to name each one separately.

Hands-On 2.6 **Set Up a New Table and Add Validation Rules**

In this exercise, you will set up a new table in the Pinnacle Pet Care database. The new table will record pet visits to the clinic. The table will contain various fields that record visit information. You will set validation rules for several of the fields to ensure accurate data entry. You will also create a Lookup Wizard field to make data entry easier.

1. Click the Tables button on the Objects bar and double-click the Create Table in Design View option.

2. Follow these steps to set up the Visits table:

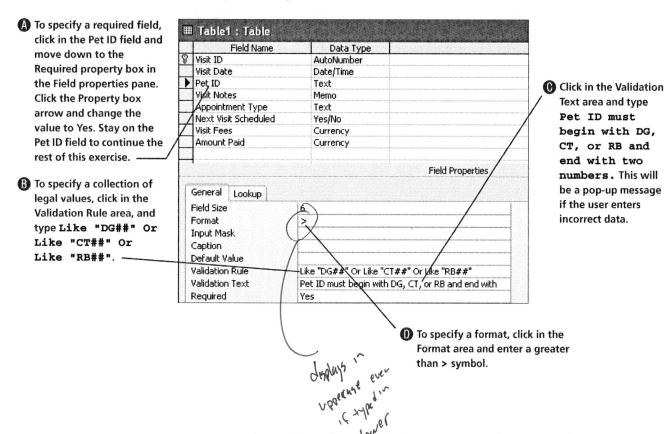

Ⓐ Type the field names shown here and choose the data types shown for each field name. Make sure you spell the field names correctly.

Ⓑ Click in the Pet ID row and set the Field Size to **6** in the Field Properties section at the bottom of the dialog box.

Ⓒ Set the Appointment Type Field Size to **25**.

Field Name	Data Type
Visit ID	AutoNumber
Visit Date	Date/Time
Pet ID	Text
Visit Notes	Memo
Appointment Type	Text
Next Visit Scheduled	Yes/No
Visit Fees	Currency
Amount Paid	Currency

Ⓔ Click in the Visit Date row and set the Format option in the Field Properties section at the bottom of the dialog box to Short Date.

Ⓓ Click in the Visit ID row then click the Primary Key 🔑 button on the Access toolbar. A key icon will appear indicating that Visit ID is the primary key. The primary key uniquely identifies each record in the table.

3. Follow these steps to set up validation rules:

Ⓐ To specify a required field, click in the Pet ID field and move down to the Required property box in the Field properties pane. Click the Property box arrow and change the value to Yes. Stay on the Pet ID field to continue the rest of this exercise.

Ⓑ To specify a collection of legal values, click in the Validation Rule area, and type **Like "DG##" Or Like "CT##" Or Like "RB##"**.

Table1 : Table

Field Name	Data Type	
Visit ID	AutoNumber	
Visit Date	Date/Time	
Pet ID	Text	
Visit Notes	Memo	
Appointment Type	Text	
Next Visit Scheduled	Yes/No	
Visit Fees	Currency	
Amount Paid	Currency	

Field Properties

General | Lookup

Field Size	6
Format	>
Input Mask	
Caption	
Default Value	
Validation Rule	Like "DG##" Or Like "CT##" Or Like "RB##"
Validation Text	Pet ID must begin with DG, CT, or RB and end with
Required	Yes

Ⓒ Click in the Validation Text area and type **Pet ID must begin with DG, CT, or RB and end with two numbers.** This will be a pop-up message if the user enters incorrect data.

Ⓓ To specify a format, click in the Format area and enter a greater than > symbol.

displays in uppercase even if typed in lower

4. Make sure your table is set up properly then switch to Datasheet view.

5. Click Yes to save the table, type the name **Visits** in the Save As box, and click OK.

Working with the Lookup Wizard

A Lookup Wizard field allows the user to pick from a set of values. This reduces errors because the user isn't entering data. The wizard will walk you through the process of building the list from which the user to pick items.

 Hands-On 2.7   **Create a Lookup Wizard Field**

In this exercise, you will experiment with the Lookup Wizard.

1. Click the Design View button to switch to Design View.

2. Follow these steps to set up a Lookup Wizard field:

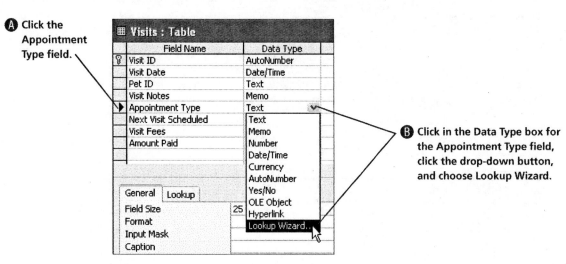

Ⓐ Click the Appointment Type field.

Ⓑ Click in the Data Type box for the Appointment Type field, click the drop-down button, and choose Lookup Wizard.

The Lookup Wizard begins.

3. Click on the I Will Type in the Values I Want option button.

4. Click the Next button to move to the next screen.

can also create a link to a table

5. Follow these steps to specify the values for your lookup field:

(A) Leave the 1 in the Number of Columns field, as you want just one column in your lookup list.

(B) Click in the first empty box and type **Scheduled**.

(C) Enter the remaining values **Walk-in**, **Promotion**, and **Follow-up** in the drop-down list. Use your arrow keys to move down the column. If you tap Enter, you will go to the next wizard screen. If that happens, just click the Back button.

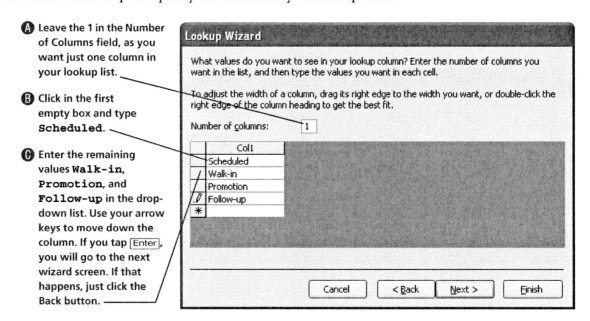

6. Click the Next button to move to the next screen. Make sure Appointment Type is listed in the window and click Finish.

7. Switch to Datasheet view and click Yes to save.

8. Tap the Tab key to bypass the Visit ID field.
You don't need to enter the Visit IDs since the Visit ID AutoNumber data type will automatically number the records as you enter data in the other fields.

9. Type **1/09/04** in the Visit Date field.

10. Tap the Tab key and type **gd13** in the Pet ID field.

11. Tap the Tab key and your message will pop up because you entered an invalid Pet ID. The message tells you how the Pet ID should look. Go back and change the Pet ID to be **dg13**.
If you typed the letters in lowercase, notice that they automatically changed to uppercase because of the format property you placed on that field.

12. Type **Dillon's owner stopped in to purchase flea treatment and schedule advanced obedience training** in the Visit Notes field.

13. Tap Tab. In the Appointment Type field you simply need to click the arrow to drop down a list of appointment types to choose from. Choose Walk-In from the list.

14. Tap Tab and place a checkmark in the box in the Next Visit Scheduled field.

15. Notice that you check the Next Visit Scheduled box to set that field to Yes and leave the box unchecked to set that field to No.

16. Tap Tab and type **60** in the Visit Fees field.

17. Tap Tab and type **60** in the Amount Paid field.

Enter Additional Records into the Visits Table

18. Enter the following visit records:

Visit ID	Visit Date	Pet ID	Visit Notes	Appointment Type	Next Visit Scheduled	Visit Fees	Amount Paid
2	1/10/04	RB23	Bugs came by for the grooming promotion	Promotion	No	45	45
3	1/10/04	CT02	Max came by for the grooming promotion	Promotion	No	45	45
4	1/11/04	CT16	Stripes was suffering from a virus	Walk-in	Yes	78	20
5	1/12/04	DG12	Wolfy came in for yearly shots	Scheduled	No	135	50
6	1/12/04	CT16	Stripes viral infection seems to have been cured	Follow-up	No	20	20
7	1/15/04	DG13	First day of obedience training	Follow-up	Yes	25	25
8	1/15/04	DG24	First day of obedience training	Follow-up	Yes	25	0
9	1/15/04	DG25	First day of obedience training	Follow-up	Yes	25	25
10	1/16/04	CT92	New patient, set up appointment for check up	Walk-in	Yes	0	0

19. Close the Visits table, saving any changes if necessary, and close Access.

20. Now continue with the end-of-lesson questions and exercises.

 **Concepts Review**

True/False Questions

1. Filters are a temporary way to view records that meet specific criteria.   TRUE   FALSE
2. To select an entire record, click anywhere in the record.   TRUE   FALSE
3. An input mask can automatically enter parenthesis ( ) around the area code of a phone number.   TRUE   FALSE
4. Changing the structure of a table will never result in lost data.   TRUE   FALSE
5. The Table Wizard is used to automate data entry in a table.   TRUE   FALSE
6. A pencil icon in the row selector indicates a new record in which you can type.   TRUE   FALSE
7. Once you are in Datasheet view, you cannot go back to the Table Design view.   TRUE   FALSE
8. To use Filter by Form you must first click on the field that contains the desired value.   TRUE   FALSE
9. The Table Wizard provides a variety of sample fields to use in a table.   TRUE   FALSE
10. Using validation rules, you can set a specific range of values allowed in the field.   TRUE   FALSE

Multiple Choice Questions

1. What is the first step you should take when deleting a record?
   a. Click in the desired record or select the record.
   b. Click the Delete Record button on the toolbar.
   c. Narrow the column width.
   d. Delete all text from the cells.

2. What is the purpose of setting a default value for a field?
   a. Data integrity—users are not allowed to enter any other value
   b. Saves time—the default value is automatically entered in new records
   c. Data entry simplification—the default value is easily entered by double-clicking
   d. None of the above

3. Filters are used to _____.
   a. establish relationships
   b. view a subset of records in a table
   c. view a list of fields in a table
   d. None of the above

4. Lookup Wizard fields help ensure data integrity by _____.
   a. automatically correcting spelling mistakes
   b. automatically capitalizing entries
   c. forcing users to choose from a list
   d. All of the above

Skill Builders

Skill Builder 2.1   Set Up a New Table

In this exercise, you will set up a new table in the Tropical Getaways database. The managers at Tropical Getaways need a table for the new Custom Travel Packages program. The table will record important information about the packages. Later you will create a form that displays information from both the Customers table and the Custom Packages table.

1. Start Access and open the Tropical Getaways database.

2. Click the Tables button on the Objects bar.

3. Double-click the Create Table in Design View option.

4. Follow these steps to set up the Custom Packages table:

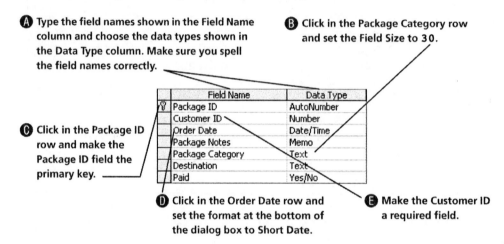

A Type the field names shown in the Field Name column and choose the data types shown in the Data Type column. Make sure you spell the field names correctly.

B Click in the Package Category row and set the Field Size to 30.

C Click in the Package ID row and make the Package ID field the primary key.

D Click in the Order Date row and set the format at the bottom of the dialog box to Short Date.

E Make the Customer ID a required field.

Field Name	Data Type
Package ID	AutoNumber
Customer ID	Number
Order Date	Date/Time
Package Notes	Memo
Package Category	Text
Destination	Text
Paid	Yes/No

5. Close the table and save it as **Custom Packages**.

Skill Builder 2.2   Use the Lookup Wizard

In this exercise, you will create a lookup field.

1. Click the Tables button on the Objects bar in the Access database window.

2. Click the Trips Table icon and open in Design View by clicking the [Design] button in the toolbar.

3. Click the Data type column for the Category field, click the drop-down arrow, and choose Lookup Wizard.

4. Choose I Will Type in the Values that I Want and click Next.

5. Leave the Column number as 1 then enter the values shown to the right into Column 1.

Col1
Adventure
Family
Leisure
Singles

6. Click Next then click Finish.

7. Click the Datasheet ▦ view button and save the table.

8. Enter the following four records into the table using the drop-down list you just created for the Category field items:

Trip ID	Customer ID	Destination	Category	Departure Date	Return Date	Cost
Fam02	4	Hawaii	Family	7/15/04	7/20/04	$3,250
Lei02	2	Swiss Alps	Leisure	5/05/04	5/23/04	$5,980
Adv03	1	Baja California	Adventure	4/17/04	4/22/04	$1,750

9. Close the table when you have finished.

Skill Builder 2.3   Experiment with the Input Mask and Validation Rules

In this exercise, you will modify a table with an input mask and you will set a format property that will function like a validation rule.

1. Open the Customers table in Design View.

2. Click on the Zip field, go down to Field Properties in the Input Mask area, and click the Build ⟦…⟧ button.
   This will open the Input Mask Wizard.

3. Choose Zip Code from the choices and click Next.

4. Click Next two more times then click Finish.

5. Click in the State field then click the Format property box and type **>** to convert all text entered in that field to capital letters.

6. Switch to Datasheet view and save the table.

7. Enter the following records. Try out your validation rule by entering the states in lowercase letters.

Customer ID	Firstname	Lastname	Address	City	State	Zip	Profile
5	Rita	Bailey	1625 Palm Street	Portland	OR	97240	Family
6	Cheryl	DeMarco	1250 Sandy Plains	Atlanta	GA	30062	Singles

8. Close the table and the database when you have finished.

 # Assessments

Assessment 2.1 Create the Events Table

In this exercise, you will create a new table in the Classic Cars database. You will add input masks and a lookup field.

1. Open the Classic Cars database.

2. Follow these guidelines to set up a new table with the structure shown in step 3:
   - Leave the field lengths of the Event Title, Sponsor, and Location fields set to 50.
   - Set the number of decimal places for the Entrance Fee field to **2**. You can do this in the Decimal Places box at the bottom of the dialog box after setting the Data type to Currency.
   - Make the Event ID field with an AutoNumber data type and designate it as the primary key.
   - Assign the name **Events** to the table.

3. Switch to Datasheet view, save the table, and enter the following records:

Event ID	Collector ID	Event Title	Event Date	Sponsor	Location	Entrance Fee	Mailing Sent	Notes
1	4	1950's Classic Chevys	9/1/04	Classic Cars Bay Chapter	San Francisco	$50	`Yes	
2	3	Early American Automobiles	10/18/04	American Collector's Association	Columbus	$25	Yes	
3	2	Classic Cars - Annual Auto Show	2/1/04	Classic Cars	Los Angeles	$10	Yes	

4. AutoFit the width of all columns and print the table.

5. Close the table when finished.

6. Open the Collectors table in Design view.

7. Place an input mask on the Zip Code field.

8. Format the State field so all characters typed into the field will convert to uppercase letters.

9. Switch to Datasheet view, save the table, and add the following records to the Collectors table:

Collector ID	Firstname	Lastname	Address	City	State	Zip	Era of Interest	Collection Size
5	Isaac	Williams	2684 Curtis Street	Denver	CO	80209	1940s	6
6	Angela	Hall	159 SW Taylor Street	Portland	OR	97205	1960s	12
7	Anthony	Jeffers	6583 F Street	San Diego	CA	92101	1930s	3

10. AutoFit the width of all columns and print the table.

11. Close table when finished.

12. Open the Cars table in Design view.

13. Create a Lookup Wizard field on the Condition field. Add the values in the example to the right to the Lookup Wizard:

Col1
Mint
Excellent
Good
Fair
Poor

14. Switch to Datasheet view, save the table, and add the following records:

Car ID	Collector ID	Year	Make	Model	Color	Condition	Value
FD02	7	30	Ford	Tudor	Black	Excellent	$35,000
CC03	6	68	Chevrolet	Camaro	Blue	Mint	$27,500
DS02	5	41	Dodge	Sedan	Maroon	Fair	$4,900

15. AutoFit the columns and print the table.

16. Close the table when you are finished.

17. Exit from Access.

Critical Thinking

Critical Thinking 2.1   Update Tables

Linda received the printed copies of the database tables and was quite satisfied; however, she has requested some changes. Open the Holmestead Realty database and update it with the following changes:

- Sharon Carter was recently married to Greg Collins. On the Contacts table, locate Sharon, change her last name, and add Greg to the spouse field.

- David Armstrong's mother is moving into the house on 14 Dover Street. Delete that listing from the Listings table.

- The Wallace's bought a new investment property at 17 Keyway Avenue. Add the property to the Listings table using the following information:

  MLS #: 52912

  Price: $175,000

  Commission Rate: 6%

  Listing Date: Today's date

  Expiration Date: 6 months from today

- Linda also wants to track the style of each home. Add a field named Style to the Listings table and enter the data in the Style column to the listings currently in the Listings table:

MLS #	Street #	Address	Style
52236	1132	Richwood Road	Bungalow
52369	6	Thoroughbred Lane	Ranch
52425	218	Wildflower Road	Contemporary
52511	403	Hawks Landing	Ranch
52524	64	Hastings Street	2 Story
52526	137	Woodbridge Lane	1 Story w/basement
52649	23	Edwards Avenue	Duplex
52650	24	Edwards Avenue	Duplex
52912	17	Keyway Avenue	2 Story

Critical Thinking 2.2   Add and Modify Tables

Linda Holmes understands that houses sell better when they feel more like homes, so she develops the Feels Like Home service. The Feels Like Home service provides maintenance, cleaning, and other services to owners who list properties with Holmestead Realty. While this service generates additional income for Linda, expenses are also involved. Linda needs to modify the Holmestead Realty database to keep track of houses that receive the Feels Like Home service, and the specific type of service they receive. Follow these guidelines to set up a table to meet these needs:

- Create a new table named **Feels Like Home**.

- Use the following field names, data types, and field properties:

Feels Like Home Table Structure

Field Name	Data Type	Field Properties
Service ID	Auto Number	Primary key
Plan	Text	
Special Instructions	Memo	
Invoice	Yes/No	
MLS #	Number	

- Save your table.

Critical Thinking 2.3   Ensure Data Integrity

Linda employs her nephew to complete data entry work for Holmestead Realty. He is a good worker but he sometimes makes errors. Linda decides to add Lookup Wizard fields to the Feels Like Home Data Entry table to help reduce data entry errors.

Follow these guidelines to create a Lookup Wizard field:

- Open the Feels Like Home table, go to the Plan field data type, and begin the Lookup Wizard. Enter the following items into the wizard to create a drop-down list:

Table Wizard Values
Plan
Set-up
Winter
Summer
Check-up

Critical Thinking 2.4   Data Entry

Use the Feels Like Home table in Datasheet view to enter the following data into the database:

Service ID	Plan	Special Instructions	Invoice	MLS #
1	Set-up	House had dogs, so clean carpet well	Y	52236
2	Set-up	Take down curtains and wash	Y	52425
3	Check-up	Check basement	Y	52236
4	Set-up	Construction debris, clean up	Y	52511

LESSON 3

Working with Forms and Reports

In this lesson, you will enhance the Pinnacle Pet Care database with forms and reports. You will create forms that will allow you to easily view, enter, and edit data in the Customers and Pets tables. You will also create reports to present your data in a variety of ways.

IN THIS LESSON

Microsoft Office Access 2003 objectives covered in this lesson

Objective Number	Skill Sets and Skills	Concept Page References	Exercise Page References
AC03S-1-8	Create forms	64, 69	65, 70, 78, 80
AC03S-1-10	Create reports	71	72–75, 81–82
AC03S-2-2	Find and move among records	65	66–67

Additional learning resources are available at labpub.com/learn/access03/

Case Study

Most of the employees at Pinnacle Pet Care have little computer experience, and they have even less experience using Microsoft Access. For this reason, Penny Johnson must make it easy for her employees to enter and extract data from the database. Penny decides to set up data entry forms that let employees enter customer and pet information. Penny also works closely with her employees to determine the types of reports they require. Penny realizes that her employees require an outstanding customer balance report that includes the customer names and telephone numbers. Another report should list the expenditures and number of visits for each pet. This report will be sorted by expenditures so customers spending the most on their pets will appear at the top of the report.

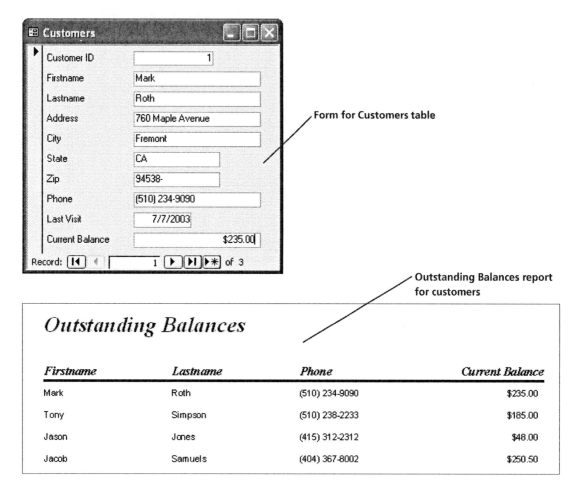

Form for Customers table

Outstanding Balances report for customers

Outstanding Balances

Firstname	Lastname	Phone	Current Balance
Mark	Roth	(510) 234-9090	$235.00
Tony	Simpson	(510) 238-2233	$185.00
Jason	Jones	(415) 312-2312	$48.00
Jacob	Samuels	(404) 367-8002	$250.50

Using Forms

In Lesson 1, Creating Tables and Entering Data and Lesson 2, Modifying and Maintaining Tables, you learned that an Access database is composed of various objects. A form is a type of object that lets you view, edit, and enter data. The benefit of a form is that it allows you to focus on a single record in the database. This is in contrast to Datasheet view, in which you can view many records at the same time. Forms are also used to create the user interface for a database. Using a form for the user to enter data allows the user to see only the record on which they are working. The following illustration shows a form for the Customers table in the Pinnacle Pet Care database.

Notice that the form displays one complete record from the database. Forms let you focus on a single customer, pet, etc.

Fields such as Phone, Last Visit, and Current Balance are automatically formatted with symbols (as they are in Datasheet view).

The form also contains navigation buttons to let you browse through the database.

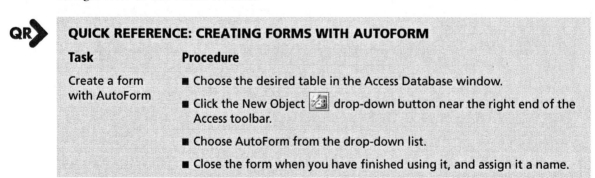

Creating Forms with AutoForm

You can use AutoForm to automatically create simple forms. AutoForm creates a form that displays all fields from a particular table. The form in the preceding illustration was created from the Customers table using AutoForm. More complex forms can be created using Form Design view or the Form Wizard.

QR

QUICK REFERENCE: CREATING FORMS WITH AUTOFORM

Task	Procedure
Create a form with AutoForm	■ Choose the desired table in the Access Database window.
	■ Click the New Object [icon] drop-down button near the right end of the Access toolbar.
	■ Choose AutoForm from the drop-down list.
	■ Close the form when you have finished using it, and assign it a name.

In this exercise, you will open the Pinnacle Pet Care database you developed in Lesson 2, Modifying and Maintaining Tables.

1. Start Access and open the Pinnacle Pet Care database.

2. Follow these steps to create a form for the Customers table:

Ⓐ **Choose the Customers table from the list of tables. You must choose the desired table before creating a form.**

Ⓑ **Click the drop-down button on the New Object button and choose Auto-Form, as shown here.**

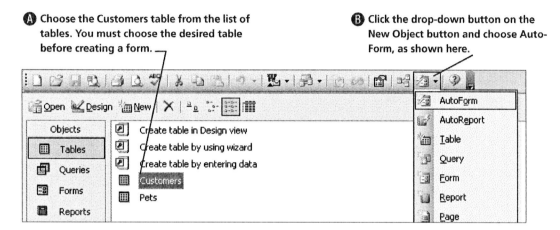

Access will create the form and display the Mark Roth record. This is because the Mark Roth record is the first record in the table.

Entering Data and Navigating Records in Forms

Forms are used for viewing and entering data one record at a time. When you enter data using a form, the data is stored in the underlying table on which that the form is based. Forms also make it easy to navigate to various records. The navigation bar at the bottom of a form lets you navigate to records in the underlying table. The form navigation bar has the same buttons that appear on the navigation bar in Datasheet view.

Go to the first record in the table.

Move forward one record.

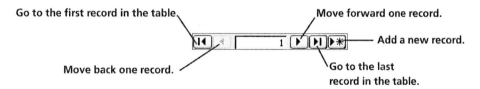

Add a new record.

Move back one record.

Go to the last record in the table.

Hands-On 3.2   Enter Data and Navigate

In this exercise, you will enter new data and practice navigating through the data.

1. Follow these steps to prepare to enter a new record:

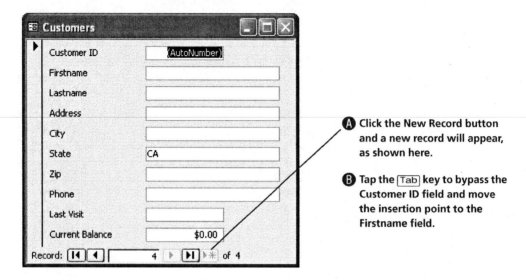

Ⓐ Click the New Record button and a new record will appear, as shown here.

Ⓑ Tap the Tab key to bypass the Customer ID field and move the insertion point to the Firstname field.

2. Enter the data shown here, using the Tab key to move from one field to the next:
Notice that you must change the entry in the State field from CA to GA. You can always change the default value for a record by typing a new value. You set the default value to CA when you created the table in Lesson 2, Modifying and Maintaining Tables. Also, the dollar sign will not appear in the Current Balance field until you go to another field or record after typing the entry in the Current Balance field.

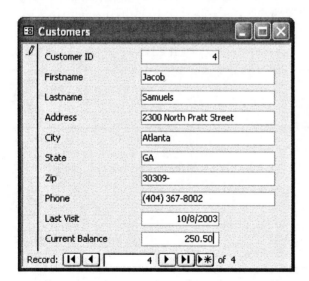

In the next few steps, you will close the form and assign a name to it. Forms use the same naming conventions as tables and all other database objects.

3. Click the Close button on the form.

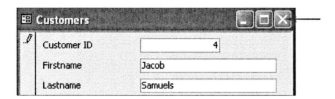

Access will ask if you want to save the form.

4. Click the Yes button and Access will propose the name Customers.

5. Click OK to accept the proposed name.

6. Follow these steps to confirm that the form has been created and to reopen the form:

Ⓐ Click the Forms button on the Objects bar and the Customers icon will appear, as shown here.

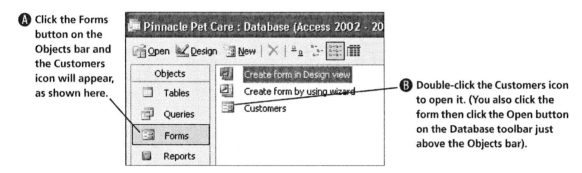

Ⓑ Double-click the Customers icon to open it. (You also click the form then click the Open button on the Database toolbar just above the Objects bar).

7. Use the navigation bar at the bottom of the form to browse through the records.
Notice that the Jacob Samuels record you just added is visible as the last record. The data you entered for Jacob Samuels has been added to the Customers table.

8. Now close the Customers form again by clicking its Close ☒ button.

Deleting and Editing Records with Forms

The Delete Record ☒ button on the Access toolbar deletes the current record displayed in a form. The record is deleted from the underlying table. You can also use a form to edit data in an underlying table. Keep in mind that you must first navigate to a record before you can edit the data or delete the record.

Hands-On 3.3   **Create a New Form and Work with Records**

In this exercise, you will create a new form for the Pets table. You will also navigate through the table and delete a record.

1. Follow these steps to create a new form for the Pets table:

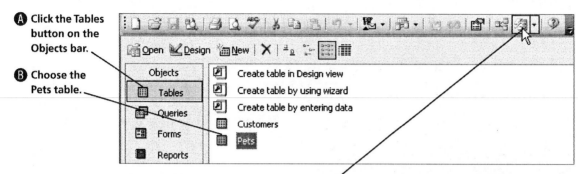

A Click the Tables button on the Objects bar.

B Choose the Pets table.

C Click the AutoForm button (not the drop-down button) to create the form. The New Objects button always displays the most recent object type created on the face of the button.

Notice that the new form is based on the fields in the Pets table.

2. Click the New Record ⏭ button on the navigation bar at the bottom of the form.

3. Enter the following records, stopping at the Breed field for Slinky the Snake:

Pet ID	Pet Name	Pet Type	Breed	Gender	Color	Date of Birth	Last Visit	Expenditures	Number of Visits	Customer ID
DG24	Ben	Dog	Terrier	Male	Black	6/1/02	10/8/03	480	3	4
DG25	Spike	Dog	Chow	Male	Brown	4/3/98	10/8/03	890	12	4
SN01	Slinky	Snake								

4. It turns out that snakes are not welcome at Pinnacle Pets so click the Delete Record ▶✕ button on the Access toolbar.

5. Click Yes to confirm the deletion of Slinky the Snake.

6. Use the navigation bar to navigate back through the records. Notice that the Ben the Dog and Spike the Dog records are still there.

7. Click the Close ✕ button on the form.

8. Click Yes when Access asks if you want to save the form.

9. Click OK on the Save As box to accept the name Pets.

10. Click the Forms button on the Objects bar to see both the Customers and Pets form icons you created.

Printing Forms

You can print the records in a table by clicking the Print button from an open form. Access will print a copy of the form with displayed data for each record in the database. This technique can be useful if you have a large number of fields in a table. Printing a datasheet with a large number of fields is often difficult because the fields can't be displayed on a single page. A form, however, will often fit on a single page. On the other hand, printing forms may not be wise if the table has a large number of records. Forms typically take a large amount of space on the printed page, and you will use a lot of paper if you print a table with many records.

Hands-On 3.4   Preview the Pets Form

In this exercise, you will use Print Preview to see how the Pets form will look if printed.

1. Click the Forms button on the Objects bar.

2. Double-click the Pets icon in the Forms section of the database window.

3. Click the Print Preview 🔍 button on the Access toolbar.

4. If necessary, maximize 🔲 the Print Preview window.

5. Click anywhere on the page in the Print Preview window to zoom in.
   Notice that a copy of the form is displayed for each record in the Pets table.

6. Use the navigation bar at the bottom of the Print Preview window to browse through the pages.
   As you can see, printing data via a form may require a lot of paper.

7. Close the Print Preview window without printing.

8. Click the Restore 🔳 button near the top-right corner of the window to restore the Pets form (not the Access program window).

9. Click the Close ⊠ button on the Pets form.

Working with the Form Wizard

The Form Wizard guides you step by step through the creation of a form. You can choose the fields to include, various layout options, and a design style for the form. Unlike the AutoForm tool, the Form Wizard gives you flexibility when setting up a form. The Form Wizard is initiated by choosing the Create Form by Using Wizard option in the Forms section of the Access database window.

Hands-On 3.5 **Create a Form Using the Form Wizard**

In this exercise, you will create a new Pets form that includes only some of the fields in the database. The Pinnacle Pet Care database window should be displayed.

1. Click the Forms button on the Objects bar.

2. Double-click the Create Form by Using Wizard option.
   In the next few steps, you will choose the fields that will be displayed on the form. It is important that you choose the fields in the order specified in this exercise.

3. Follow these steps to add fields from the Pets table:

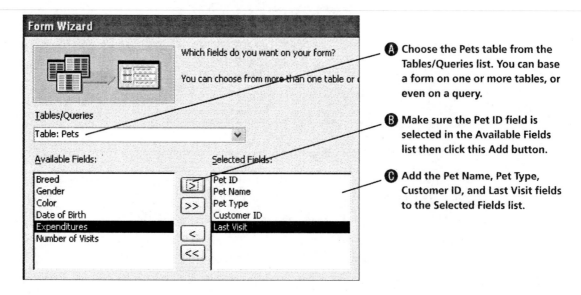

Ⓐ Choose the Pets table from the Tables/Queries list. You can base a form on one or more tables, or even on a query.

Ⓑ Make sure the Pet ID field is selected in the Available Fields list then click this Add button.

Ⓒ Add the Pet Name, Pet Type, Customer ID, and Last Visit fields to the Selected Fields list.

4. Click the Next button to display the next wizard screen.

5. With the Columnar option chosen, click the Next button.

6. Choose Standard as the style then click the Next button.

7. Type the name **Pets Last Visit** as the title and click the Finish button.
   Access will create the form as shown to the right; however, your form may have a slightly different layout. Notice that the form displays the data for Max the Cat and that there are nine records.

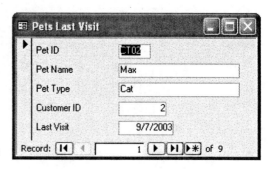

8. Use the record navigation buttons at the bottom of the form to browse through the records in the Pets Last Visit form.

9. Close the form.

Using Reports

You can create reports to present data in a printed format. You can specify the fields to include in reports and you can format reports using built-in report styles. In Hands-On 3.6, you will create the following report. Notice that the report lists just four fields from the Customers table.

Outstanding Balances

Firstname	Lastname	Phone	Current Balance
Mark	Roth	(510) 234-9090	$235.00
Tony	Simpson	(510) 238-2233	$185.00
Jason	Jones	(415) 312-2312	$48.00
Jacob	Samuels	(404) 367-8002	$250.50

Complexity of Reports

In this lesson, you will use the Report Wizard to create simple reports. However, Access reports can be quite complex. For example, reports can include calculated fields that sum columns of numbers and grouping levels to organize records in logical groups.

AutoReport and the Report Wizard

In the previous Hands-On exercises, you used AutoForm to create forms. AutoForm created a form using all fields from a table and the Form Wizard allowed you to select certain fields to be used on a form. Reports usually require a subset of a table's fields. For example, the report shown in the previous illustration uses just four fields from the Customers table. AutoReport has limited use because it inserts all fields from a table into a report. Fortunately, Access provides a Report Wizard that gives you flexibility when setting up reports. The Report Wizard lets you choose the fields to include in the report. The Report Wizard also lets you specify various formatting options.

QUICK REFERENCE: USING THE REPORT WIZARD

Task	Procedure
Use the Report Wizard to create a report	■ Click the Reports button on the Objects bar in the Database window.
	■ Double-click the Create Report by Using Wizard option. You can also click the New button on the Access Database toolbar then choose Report Wizard from the dialog box.
	■ Choose the desired table or query on which you wish to base the report from the Tables/Queries list and click OK.
	■ Follow the Report Wizard steps to create the desired report.

Previewing and Printing Reports

The button appears on the Access Database toolbar whenever the Reports button is pressed on the Objects bar and a report is chosen. You can open the report in Print Preview mode by clicking the Preview button. The Print Preview window functions the same way with reports as it does with other objects.

FROM THE KEYBOARD

[Ctrl]+[P] to display
Print dialog box

The Print ⊜ button can be used to print reports directly from the Database window. The Print button also appears on the Print Preview toolbar when a report is chosen. You can print all pages of a report by clicking the Print button. You must use the File→Print command to display the Print dialog box if you want to print a range of pages or set other print options.

🖰 Hands-On 3.6   Use the Report Wizard

In this exercise you will create a new report using the Report Wizard.

Create an Outstanding Balances Report

1. Follow these steps to launch the Report Wizard:

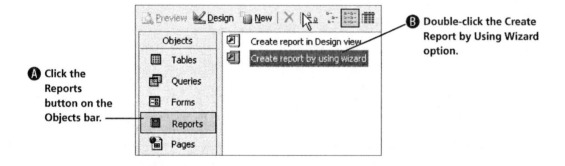

A Click the Reports button on the Objects bar.

B Double-click the Create Report by Using Wizard option.

2. Follow these steps to choose the Customers table as the basis for the report and to add the Firstname field to the Selected Fields list:

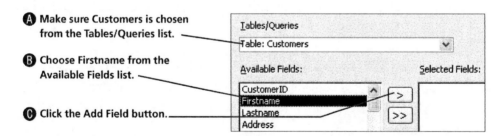

A Make sure Customers is chosen from the Tables/Queries list.

B Choose Firstname from the Available Fields list.

C Click the Add Field button.

3. Now add the Lastname, Phone, and Current Balance fields. The completed Selected Fields list is shown to the right.

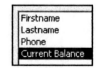

4. Click Next to display the Grouping Levels screen.

5. Click Next to bypass the Grouping Levels screen and display the Sort Order screen.

6. Click Next to bypass the Sort Order screen and display the Layout screen. Make sure the layout options are set as shown in the following illustration.

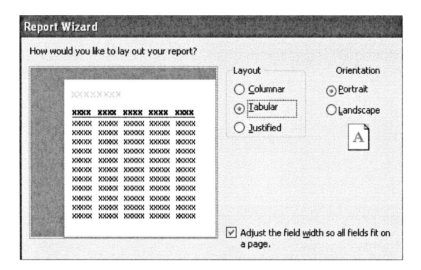

7. Click Next to display the Style screen.

8. Choose Corporate, click Next, and follow these steps to set the final report options:

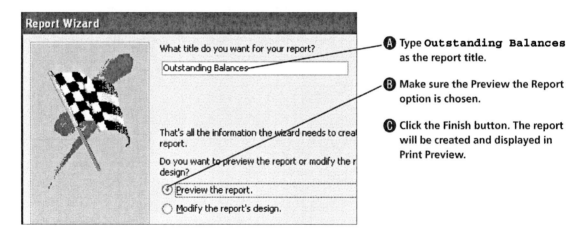

A Type **Outstanding Balances** as the report title.

B Make sure the Preview the Report option is chosen.

C Click the Finish button. The report will be created and displayed in Print Preview.

9. If necessary, maximize the Print Preview window by clicking its Maximize ▣ button.

10. Zoom in or out on the report by clicking the mouse pointer anywhere on it.

Outstanding Balances

Firstname	Lastname	Phone	Current Balance
Mark	Roth	(510) 234-9090	$235.00
Tony	Simpson	(510) 238-2233	$185.00
Jason	Jones	(415) 312-2312	$48.00
Jacob	Samuels	(404) 367-8002	$250.50

11. Click the Design view button on the left end of the Print Preview toolbar.
    The report will display in Design view with a report header, page header, detail section, etc. In Design view, you can change the position of objects, add, and remove objects, and change the properties of objects. However, you won't work in Design view at this time.

12. Click the Print Preview button to switch back to Print Preview.

13. Feel free to print the report by clicking the Print button on the Print Preview toolbar.

14. Choose File→Close from the menu bar to close the report.
    The Report will automatically be assigned the name Outstanding Balances, and an Outstanding Balances icon will appear in the Reports section of the database window. As you can see from this example, creating simple reports is quite easy if you use the Report Wizard. You will now continue with the remainder of this exercise, where you will create a report to accompany the Pets table.

Create a Pets Report

15. With the Reports button pressed on the Objects bar, double-click the Create Report by Using Wizard option.

16. Choose the Pets table from the Tables/Queries list.

17. Add the Pet Name, Pet Type, Expenditures, and Number of Visits fields to the Selected Fields list as shown to the right.

18. Click the Finish button to accept all of the remaining default settings. The completed report shown in the following illustration will appear.

Selected Fields:

Pet Name
Pet Type
Expenditures
Number of Visits

Pets

Pet Name	Pet Type	Expenditures	Number of Visits
Wolfy	Dog	$450.00	7
Dillon	Dog	$150.55	3
Bugs	Rabbit	$600.50	4
Max	Cat	$1,450.55	20
Stripes	Cat	$450.00	9
Fetch	Dog	$345.00	3
Tony	Cat	$145.00	6
Ben	Dog	$480.00	3
Spike	Dog	$890.00	12

19. Notice the alignment of the fields within the columns.
Fields have the same left or right alignment in a report as they do in the table on which the report is based.

20. Close the report with the File→Close command.
The Reports section should now have an Outstanding Balance report and a Pets report.

Managing Objects

Occasionally you will have to copy, delete, or rename objects in your database. The ability to copy objects is helpful for making duplicates of the object for a backup or to bring a copy of an object to another database file. Sometimes you may finish up a wizard without realizing you didn't give an object the name you prefer. In that case, the ability to rename an object is extremely helpful.

Copying Objects

You can copy tables, forms, reports, and other types of objects. Objects can be copied and pasted into the same database, to a different database, and to other applications. Copying an object to the same database can be useful if you intend to modify the object. By making a copy, you will have a backup of the object in case the original is damaged. Objects are copied using the Copy and Paste buttons on the Access toolbar.

FROM THE KEYBOARD
Ctrl+C to copy
Ctrl+V to paste

Deleting Objects

Objects can also be deleted from an Access database. However, you must be careful when deleting objects because they will be permanently deleted from the database. Deleting objects can be useful, especially when using wizards and tools like AutoForm. If you make a mistake or are unhappy with the results of an automated process, you can delete the object and start over. You delete an object by choosing the desired object in the database window and issuing the Edit→Delete command. You can also click the Delete button on the Access Database toolbar.

FROM THE KEYBOARD
Delete to delete selected object

Renaming Objects

Sometimes you will need to rename an object, either because it was given the default name that doesn't adequately describe what the object represents or contains, or it was given an inadequate name. For instance, if you don't give a table a name it will be called Table1. It isn't difficult to rename an object but you need to be careful not to rename objects that other objects are using. If you create a report based on a table and you rename the table, the report will no longer be able to find the data. You rename an object by choosing the object in the database window and choosing Edit→ Rename or by right-clicking on the object and choosing Rename.

FROM THE KEYBOARD
F2 to edit object name

Hands-On 3.7   Manage Objects

In this exercise, you will practice copying, deleting, and renaming objects.

Copy the Report

1. Choose the Pets icon in the Reports section of the database window.

2. Click the Copy button on the Access toolbar.

3. Click the Paste button on the toolbar and the Paste As box will appear.

4. Type the name **Copy of Pets** in the Paste As box and click OK.
   The Copy of Pets report will appear in the Reports section.

5. Double-click the Copy of Pets report, and it will open.
   Notice that this report is identical to the Pets report.

6. Close the report with the File→Close command.

Delete the Report

7. Make sure the Copy of Pets report is chosen.

8. Click the Delete X button on the database toolbar.

9. Click Yes to confirm the deletion.
   Keep in mind that you can delete a report (or other object) whenever you want to "get a fresh start." This technique is useful when using wizards and other automated tools. You may need to use this technique in the Skill Builder and Assessment exercises on the following pages. You will create several reports in these exercises that are more complex than the reports you just created. If you make a mistake, remember to delete the report and recreate it with the Report Wizard.

Rename the Report

10. Right-click on the Pets icon in the Reports section of the database window.

11. Click the Rename option, type **Expenditures** to replace the word Pets, and tap the Enter key.
    Renaming the report will help you to identify what the report is about just by looking at the title.

12. Close the Pinnacle Pet Care database with the File→Close command.

Concepts Review

True/False Questions

1. Forms can be used to enter data in tables.   TRUE   FALSE

2. The main benefit of forms is that they allow you to view several records simultaneously.   TRUE   FALSE

3. The navigation buttons at the bottom of a form can be used to move between records.   TRUE   FALSE

4. Forms do not display currency symbols ($) and other formatting characters.   TRUE   FALSE

5. AutoForm creates a form for the table selected in the Tables section of the Access window.   TRUE   FALSE

6. The Report Wizard lets you choose the fields you wish to include in a report.   TRUE   FALSE

7. Reports can be printed.   TRUE   FALSE

8. The Report Wizard lets you choose Portrait or Landscape orientations.   TRUE   FALSE

9. Reports can be used to enter data.   TRUE   FALSE

10. An object can be copied and then pasted to a different database.   TRUE   FALSE

Multiple Choice Questions

1. Which of the following statements about forms is true?
   a. Forms can be used to enter records into a table.
   b. Forms can be used to browse the records in a table.
   c. Forms let you focus on one record at a time.
   d. All of the above

2. Which of the following commands can you issue through the navigation buttons on a form?
   a. Add a new record
   b. Delete a record
   c. Change the size of a field
   d. All of the above

3. Which of the following statements about the Report Wizard is true?
   a. The Report Wizard lets you choose Portrait or Landscape orientation.
   b. The Report Wizard lets you choose the fields to include in a report.
   c. The Report Wizard lets you choose a title for the report.
   d. All of the above

4. The Report Wizard is initiated from which section of the database window?
   a. Tables
   b. Reports
   c. Forms
   d. All of the above

Skill Builders

Skill Builder 3.1   Create Forms

In this exercise, you will open the Tropical Getaways database you developed in Lesson 2, Modifying and Maintaining Tables. You will continue to enhance this database as you progress through the Skill Builder exercises in this course.

The Access window should be open from the previous exercise, and all databases should be closed.

Create a Form for the Customers Table

1. Click the Open 📂 button on the Access toolbar, navigate to your file storage location, and open the Tropical Getaways database.

2. Make sure the Tables button is pressed on the Objects bar.

3. Choose the Customers table, click the New Object 🔲 ▾ drop-down button, and choose AutoForm.
   Access will create the following form. The form uses all of the fields in the Customers table.

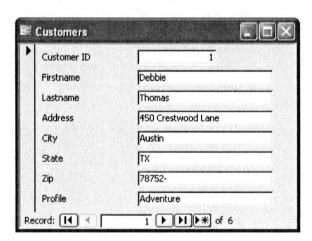

4. Click the New Record ▶⁎ button on the form's navigation bar then add the following records:

Customer ID	Firstname	Lastname	Address	City	State	Zip	Profile
7	Victor	Thomas	2311 Wilmont Street	Danvers	MA	01923	Adventure
8	Lisa	Simms	100 Westside Drive	Batavia	NY	14020	Leisure
9	Ted	Carter	250 Smith Street	Charlton	MA	01507	Family

5. Click the Close ⊠ button on the form and choose Yes when Access asks you to save the form.

6. Click OK to accept the proposed name Customers.

Create a Form for the Trips Table

7. Use AutoForm to create a form for the Trips table.

8. Use the form to add the following records to the Trips table:
   Notice the drop-down list in the Category field, which allows you to pick from a list instead of having to type the entry.

Trip ID	Customer ID	Destination	Category	Departure Date	Return Date	Cost
Adv04	1	Swiss Alps	Adventure	10/10/04	11/5/04	$3,500
Adv05	5	Rocky Mountains	Adventure	5/6/04	5/22/04	$2,190
Adv06	5	Baja California	Adventure	8/8/04	8/18/04	$2,900
Lei03	6	Hawaii	Leisure	2/5/04	2/15/04	$4,500
Fam03	7	Hawaii	Family	3/7/04	3/15/04	$5,300

9. Close the form and save it with the proposed name Trips.
   Leave the Tropical Getaways database open. You will continue to use it in the next exercise.

Skill Builder 3.2   Create Forms with the Form Wizard

In this exercise, you will use the Form Wizard to create a new form.

1. Click the Forms button on the Objects bar in the database window.

2. Double-click the Create Form by Using Wizard option.

3. Follow these steps to add the fields from the Customers table:

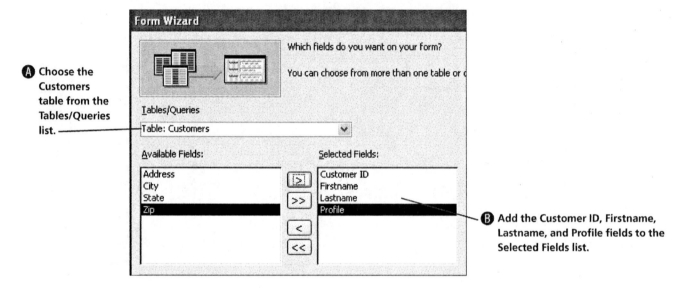

Ⓐ Choose the Customers table from the Tables/Queries list.

Ⓑ Add the Customer ID, Firstname, Lastname, and Profile fields to the Selected Fields list.

4. Click the Next button to display the next wizard screen.

5. With the Columnar option chosen, click the Next button.

6. Choose Standard as the style and click the Next button.

7. Type the name **Customer Profile** as the title then click the Finish button.
   Access will create the form shown to the right; however, your form may have a slightly different layout.

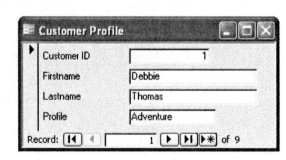

8. Close the form.

Skill Builder 3.3   Create Reports

In this exercise, you will create reports for the Tropical Getaways database. You will use the sort option in the Report Wizard to sort the records in the reports.

Create a Customer Profiles Report

1. Click the Reports button on the Objects bar.

2. Double-click the Create Report by Using Wizard option.

3. Choose Customers from the Tables/Queries list.

4. Add the Firstname, Lastname, State, and Profile fields to the Selected Fields list.

5. Click the Next button twice to display the Sorting screen.

6. Click the drop-down button on the first sorting box and choose State, as shown to the right.

1	State	⌄	Ascending

   This will group all records with the same state in the report. Notice that you can set additional sort options. For example, imagine that you have a large database and want the records sorted first by state then by zip code within the states. In this situation, you would set the second sort key to zip code.

7. Click the Next button twice to display the Report Style screen.

8. Choose the Soft Gray style and click Next.

9. Type the name **Customer Profiles by State** in the title box of the last screen.

10. Click the Finish button to complete the report.
    Your completed report should match the following illustration. Notice that the State field appears first in the report and the records for each state are grouped. The State field appears first because you sorted on that field.

Customer Profiles by State

State	Firstname	Lastname	Profile
GA	Cheryl	DeMarco	Singles
MA	Ted	Carter	Family
MA	Victor	Thomas	Adventure
NY	Lisa	Simms	Leisure
NY	Wilma	Boyd	Leisure
OR	Rita	Bailey	Family
TX	Alice	Simpson	Family
TX	Ted	Wilkins	Adventure
TX	Debbie	Thomas	Adventure

11. Close the report when you have finished viewing it.
Access will automatically name the report Customer Profiles by State.

Create a Report for the Trips Table

12. Now create the following report for the Trips table. You will need to start the Report Wizard and choose the appropriate fields from the Trips table. Also, sort the report on the Category field, choose the Soft Gray style, and use the report title Trips by Category.

Trips by Category

Category	Destination	Cost
Adventure	Baja California	$2,900.00
Adventure	Rocky Mountains	$2,190.00
Adventure	Swiss Alps	$3,500.00
Adventure	Baja California	$1,750.00
Adventure	Amazon Jungle Trek	$7,765.00
Adventure	Kenyan Safari	$6,600.00
Family	Hawaii	$5,300.00
Family	Hawaii	$3,250.00
Family	Orlando	$3,400.00
Leisure	Hawaii	$4,500.00
Leisure	Swiss Alps	$5,980.00
Leisure	Caribbean Cruise	$2,390.00

13. Close the report when you have finished viewing it.
Your Tropical Getaways database should now have two reports: Customer Profiles by State and Trips by Category.

14. Use the File→Close command to close the database. The Access program window should remain open.

# Assessments

Assessment 3.1 Create Forms and Reports

In this exercise, you will open the Classic Cars database you developed in Lesson 2, Modifying and Maintaining Tables. You will continue to enhance this database as you progress through the Assessment exercises in this course.

1. Open the Classic Cars database.

2. Use AutoForm to create the following form for the Collectors table.

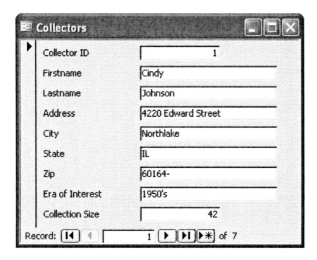

3. Use the form to enter the following new record into the Collectors table:

Collector ID	Firstname	Lastname	Address	City	State	Zip	Era of Interest	Collection Size
8	Jake	Johnson	840 Edgewood Drive	Arcadia	FL	33821	1920s	3

4. Close the form and save it with the proposed name Collectors.

5. Use AutoForm to create the following form for the Cars table.

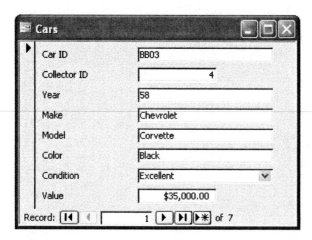

6. Use the form to enter the following new records into the table:

Car ID	Collector ID	Year	Make	Model	Color	Condition	Value
CJ04	1	48	Packard	Custom Eight Sedan	White	Fair	$15,000
JJ01	5	27	Ford	Model A	Black	Mint	$75,000
BB04	4	57	Chevrolet	Corvette	Red	Excellent	$42,000

7. Close the form and save it with the proposed name Cars.

8. Create the following report for the Collectors table. The report sorts the records by the Era of Interest field and it uses the Compact style. Also notice the title is Era of Interest.

Era of Interest

Era of Interest	Firstname	Lastname	Collection Size
1920s	Jake	Johnson	3
1930s	Anthony	Jeffers	3
1940s	Isaac	Williams	6
1950s	Bob	Barker	7
1950s	Cindy	Johnson	42
1960s	Angela	Hall	12
1960s	Tammy	Olson	6
Early 1900s	Ed	Larkson	34

9. Print the report then close it.

10. Create the following report for the Cars table. When adding the fields in the first Report Wizard screen, you will need to add them in the order shown on the report. For example, add the Model field first, the Year field second, the Condition field third, etc. This report is sorted on the Model field and it uses the Compact style.

Models Report

Model	Year	Condition	Color	Value
Camaro	68	Mint	Blue	$27,500.00
Corvette	57	Excellent	Red	$42,000.00
Corvette	58	Excellent	Black	$35,000.00
Corvette	62	Excellent	Blue	$30,000.00
Corvette	58	Mint	Red and white	$65,000.00
Custom Eight Sedan	48	Fair	White	$15,000.00
Model A	27	Mint	Black	$75,000.00
Sedan	41	Fair	Maroon	$4,900.00
Thunderbird	59	Good	Tan	$20,000.00
Tudor	30	Excellent	Black	$35,000.00

11. Print the report then close it.

12. Close the Classic Cars database when you have finished.

Critical Thinking

Critical Thinking 3.1   Create Forms

Linda Holmes has been working with her new database for some time and she has come to realize that working in Datasheet view can be awkward. Linda has asked you to set up a form that can be used for entering data and browsing records. Follow these guidelines to set up the form:

- Open the Holmestead Realty database you developed in Lesson 2, Modifying and Maintaining Tables. You will continue to develop this database as you progress through the Critical Thinking exercises in this course.

- Use the AutoForm tool to create a form for the Contacts table.

- Name the form **Contacts Data Entry**.

- Use the new form to add the contacts in the following table to the database. If a field is empty in the table then leave it empty on the form as well.

Seller ID	Firstname	Lastname	Spousename	Address	City	ST	Zip	Phone	Contact Type
7	Mark	Thames		76 Haywood Road	Asheville	NC	28801	(828) 252-5676	Primary Residence
8	Cindy	Johnson		24 Maple Drive	Black Mountain	NC	28711	(828) 686-3511	Trustee

It turns out that Susan Jones' name was spelled incorrectly in the Contacts table. She spells her first name Suzanne. She is the spouse of Jeff Jones. In your new form, use the Find feature to locate Jeff Jones' record in the Contacts table and make the correction.

Linda Holmes was so pleased with the form you created that she has asked you to create a form for the Listings table. Follow these guidelines to set up the form:

- Use the AutoForm tool and name the form **Listings Data Entry**.

- Use the form to add the following listings to the Listings table:

MLS #	Street #	Address	Price	Listing Date	Expiration Date	Commission Range	Seller ID	Style
52125	76	Haywood Road	$325,000	7/14/04	2/14/05	5%	7	3 Story
52345	625	Brevard Road	$135,000	8/5/04	12/5/05	6%	8	Ranch

You have just been informed that the Woodbridge Lane listing has expired. Use the Listings Data Entry form to remove this listing from the Listings table.

Critical Thinking 3.2 Create Reports

Linda Holmes has promised all of her sellers that she will call them at least once a week. She realizes that to do this she will need a report that displays contact information for her sellers. Follow these guidelines to create the necessary report:

■ Use the Report Wizard to set up the report. The report should extract data from the Contacts table.

■ Display the Firstname, Lastname, Spousename, Contact Type, and Phone fields on the report in the same order listed here.

■ Accept all of the default Report Wizard settings except for the report style: Choose the Casual report style instead.

Name the report **Contact Phone List** and print it when finished.

Linda was caught off guard by the expiration of the Woodbridge listing and she doesn't want this to happen again. Follow these guidelines to create a report that tracks listing expiration dates:

■ Use the Report Wizard to set up the report. The report should extract data from the Listings table.

■ Display the MLS #, Street #, Address, Price, and Expiration Date fields on the report in the same order listed here.

■ Accept all of the default Report Wizard settings except for the sort order and report style. Sort the report in ascending order on the Expiration Date field and choose the Casual report style.

■ Name the report **Expiration Date List** and print it when finished.

■ Save your changes and exit from Access.

LESSON 4

Getting Answers with Queries

In this lesson, you will learn how to set up and use queries. Queries are an essential part of any Access database. They allow you to extract and combine data from tables. You will learn how to specify criteria in queries to extract only the records you desire. You will create calculated fields; work with statistical functions; and sort, group, and print query results.

Microsoft Office Access 2003 objectives covered in this lesson

Objective Number	Skill Sets and Skills	Concept Page References	Exercise Page References
AC03S-3-4	Format datasheets	107	108
AC03S-3-5	Sort records	95, 97	96–98

Case Study

The staff at Pinnacle Pet Care has used their new database for some time and now they want answers to a variety of questions. For example:

- What is the current balance of each customer in California?

- Which customers have a current balance greater than $200?

- Which customers in California have a current balance greater than $200?

- What is the average amount of money that customers spend on cats and dogs?

Penny Johnson sets up queries in the Pinnacle Pet Care database to answer these questions. The following illustrations show a query, the Customers table, and the resulting recordset.

Field:	FirstName	LastName	Phone	Current Balance
Table:	Customers	Customers	Customers	Customers
Sort:				Descending
Show:	☑	☑	☑	☑
Criteria:				>200

A query contains fields and criteria used to select records from a table.

Customer ID	Firstname	Lastname	Address	City	State	Zip	Phone	Last Visit	Current Balance
1	Mark	Roth	760 Maple Avenue	Fremont	CA	94538-	(510) 234-9090	7/7/2003	$235.00
2	Tony	Simpson	312 York Lane	Richmond	CA	94804-	(510) 238-2233	9/7/2003	$185.00
3	Jason	Jones	2233 Crystal Street	San Mateo	CA	94403-	(415) 312-2312	7/15/2003	$48.00
4	Jacob	Samuels	2300 North Pratt Str	Atlanta	GA	30309-	(404) 367-8002	10/8/2003	$250.50

FirstName	LastName	Phone	Current Balance
Mark	Roth	(510) 234-9090	$235.00
Jacob	Samuels	(404) 367-8002	$250.50

Access produces a recordset when the query is run.

What Are Queries?

Queries are an essential part of any Access database. Most people use queries to get answers to questions and to extract data from one or more tables. When you run a query, Access creates a temporary table using the fields and criteria you specify in the query. The temporary table is known as a recordset. The recordset is composed of data from one or more tables in your database. A query's recordset can even be used as the basis for forms and reports. Thus, queries give you the ability to produce forms and reports using data from multiple tables.

Working with Select Queries

Select queries are the most common type of query. They let you selectively extract data from one or more tables in a database. When designing select queries, you specify the fields you wish to include in the recordset. You can also specify criteria used to select records from the table(s) in your database. The following illustrations show the Customers table from the Pinnacle Pet Care database and the resulting recordset. Take a few moments to study the illustrations.

Customer ID	Firstname	Lastname	Address	City	State	Zip	Phone	Last Visit	Current Balance
1	Mark	Roth	760 Maple Avenue	Fremont	CA	94538-	(510) 234-9090	7/7/2003	$235.00
2	Tony	Simpson	312 York Lane	Richmond	CA	94804-	(510) 238-2233	9/7/2003	$185.00
3	Jason	Jones	2233 Crystal Street	San Mateo	CA	94403-	(415) 312-2312	7/15/2003	$48.00
4	Jacob	Samuels	2300 North Pratt Str	Atlanta	GA	30309-	(404) 367-8002	10/8/2003	$250.50

FirstName	LastName	Phone	Current Balance
Mark	Roth	(510) 234-9090	$235.00
Jacob	Samuels	(404) 367-8002	$250.50

A query is run that instructs Access to only choose the Firstname, Lastname, Phone, and Current Balance fields from the Customers table for those customers with a Current Balance >$200.

The query produces the recordset shown here. Notice that the recordset only includes the specified fields for customers who have a Current Balance of >$200.

Setting Up Queries

You can use the Query Wizard to assist you in setting up queries, or you can set them up yourself using the Query Design grid. The Design grid gives you complete flexibility in determining the fields, criteria, and other options that you wish to use in the query. The following Quick Reference table describes how to display the Query window and how to add tables to the query. You must add table(s) to the Query window in order to use the desired fields from the table(s) in the query.

QUICK REFERENCE: ADDING TABLES TO THE QUERY WINDOW	
Task	**Procedure**
Add a table to the Query window	■ Open the desired database, and make sure the Queries button is pressed on the Objects bar.
	■ Double-click the Create Query in Design View option.
	■ Choose a table that you want the query to extract data from in the Show Table box and click Add.
	■ Add any other tables from which you wish to extract data.
	■ Click the Close button on the Show Table box.

 Hands-On 4.1   **Set Up a Query**

In this exercise, you will begin setting up a query. You will display the Query window and you will add the Customers table in the Pinnacle Pet Care database to it.

Display the Query window

1. Start Access and open the Pinnacle Pet Care database.

2. Click the Queries button on the Objects bar.

3. Double-click the Create Query in Design View option.
   The Query window will appear and the Show Table dialog box will be displayed. The Show Table dialog box lets you choose the table(s) you wish to use in the query. In this exercise, you will add just the Customers table to the Query window.

4. Choose Customers and click the Add button.
   A Customers field list will appear above the Design grid. The field names in the list are taken from the Customers table. In a moment, you will use the Customers field list to add fields to the query.

TIP! *You can also double-click the table name to add it to a query.*

5. Click the Close button on the Show Table dialog box.
   You won't be using the other tables in this exercise.

Set Up the Window

6. Make sure both the Access window and the Query window are maximized 🔲 within the Access window.

7. Follow these steps to adjust the size of the Design grid and the Customers field list:

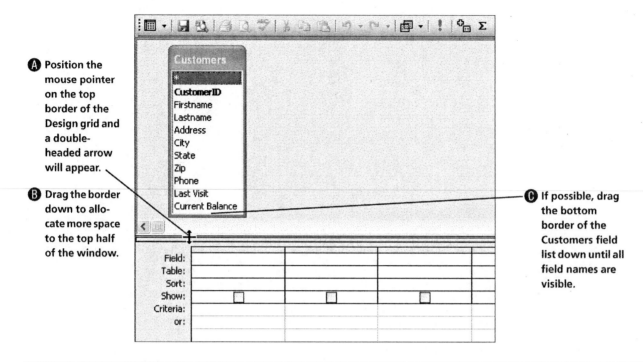

Ⓐ Position the mouse pointer on the top border of the Design grid and a double-headed arrow will appear.

Ⓑ Drag the border down to allocate more space to the top half of the window.

Ⓒ If possible, drag the bottom border of the Customers field list down until all field names are visible.

Working with the Query Design Grid

The Design grid appears when you begin setting up a new query. The Design grid lets you specify the fields to include in the query. You can also use the Design grid to specify criteria and other parameters that affect the query recordset. The following illustration shows the Design grid and the recordset for the sample query shown. You will develop the query shown in the illustration as you progress through the next few exercises.

The Table row indicates the table from which each field is taken. In this example, all fields are taken from the Customers table.

Fields such as Firstname, Lastname, Phone, and Current Balance are added to the columns of the Design grid. These fields will be displayed in the recordset.

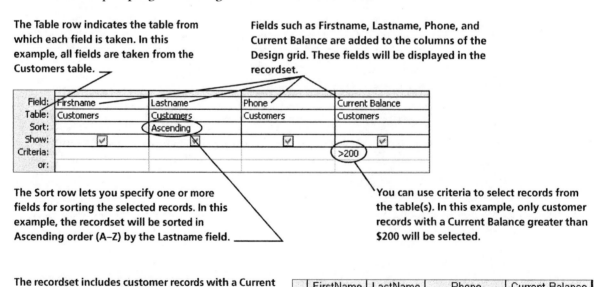

The Sort row lets you specify one or more fields for sorting the selected records. In this example, the recordset will be sorted in Ascending order (A–Z) by the Lastname field.

You can use criteria to select records from the table(s). In this example, only customer records with a Current Balance greater than $200 will be selected.

The recordset includes customer records with a Current Balance greater than $200. Only the fields specified in the query appear in the recordset.

FirstName	LastName	Phone	Current Balance
Mark	Roth	(510) 234-9090	$235.00
Jacob	Samuels	(404) 367-8002	$250.50

Adding Fields to the Design Grid

The first step in defining a query is to add fields to the Design grid. The fields you add to the Design grid will appear in the recordset. Once you have added fields to the Design grid, you can specify sorting options, criteria, and other options that affect the recordset. The following Quick Reference table describes the techniques you can use to add fields to the Design grid.

QUICK REFERENCE: ADDING FIELDS TO THE QUERY DESIGN GRID

Technique	Description
Double-click	You can add a single field to the Design grid by double-clicking the desired field in the field list.
Drop-down list	You can add a single field by clicking in a field cell, clicking the drop-down button that appears, and choosing the desired field from the drop-down menu.
Drag	You can add a single field or multiple fields to the Design grid by dragging them from a field list to the desired cell in the Design grid. You can select multiple fields prior to dragging by pressing and holding the [Ctrl] key while clicking the desired field names in the field list.
All fields	You can add all fields to the Design grid by double-clicking the asterisk (*) symbol at the top of the desired field list.

 Hands-On 4.2   Add Fields to the Design Grid

In this exercise, you will add fields to the Design grid.

1. Follow these steps to add the Firstname field to the Design grid:

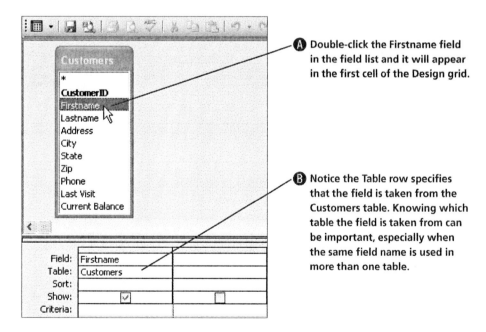

A Double-click the Firstname field in the field list and it will appear in the first cell of the Design grid.

B Notice the Table row specifies that the field is taken from the Customers table. Knowing which table the field is taken from can be important, especially when the same field name is used in more than one table.

2. Now add the Lastname, Phone, and Current Balance fields to the Design grid by double-clicking them on the field name list. When you have finished adding the filed, the Design grid should match the following illustration.

Field:	FirstName	LastName	Phone	Current Balance
Table:	Customers	Customers	Customers	Customers
Sort:				
Show:	☑	☑	☑	☑
Criteria:				
or:				

Removing Fields from the Design Grid

You can remove fields from the Design grid by clicking in the desired column and choosing Edit→Delete Columns from the menu bar. You may need to remove fields from time to time as you develop queries. Remember to use this technique if you make a mistake and add an incorrect field to the Design grid.

 Hands-On 4.3 **Delete a Field**

In this exercise, you will practice deleting a field from the Design grid.

1. Click anywhere in the Current Balance column in the Design grid.

2. Choose Edit→Delete Columns from the menu bar and the field will be removed.

3. Follow these steps to reinsert the Current Balance field using the drop-down list technique:

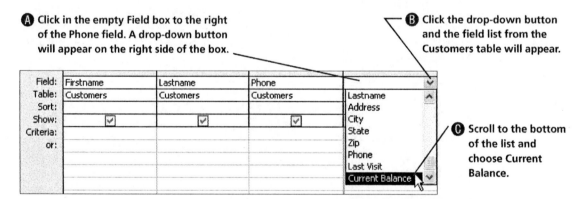

Ⓐ Click in the empty Field box to the right of the Phone field. A drop-down button will appear on the right side of the box.

Ⓑ Click the drop-down button and the field list from the Customers table will appear.

Ⓒ Scroll to the bottom of the list and choose Current Balance.

The Current Balance field should be returned to the grid. As you can see, there are several ways to add fields to the Design grid. Once again, feel free to remove fields from the Design grid whenever you make a mistake or wish to change the order of the fields in the grid.

Running Queries

You can run a query by clicking the Run ⚡ button on the Access toolbar. When you run a select query, Access selects records and fields from tables in your database and displays the recordset. You can navigate through the recordset or print it if desired. The recordset will always reflect the current data stored in the database.

Editing Data in a Recordset

When you run a select query, the recordset is connected to the underlying table(s) on which the query is based. If you edit data in the recordset, the data in the underlying tables is changed as well. However, most select queries are only used for viewing selective data.

 Hands-On 4.4   Run the Query

In this exercise, you will run the query.

1. Click the Run ⚡ button on the Access toolbar.
   The query will run and the following recordset will appear. Keep in mind that your query is quite basic. It simply displays four fields from each record in the Customers table.

FirstName	LastName	Phone	Current Balance
Mark	Roth	(510) 234-9090	$235.00
Tony	Simpson	(510) 238-2233	$185.00
Jason	Jones	(415) 312-2312	$48.00
Jacob	Samuels	(404) 367-8002	$250.50

2. Now continue with the next topic, in which you will learn how to sort query results.

Sorting Query Results

You can instruct Access to sort the rows in a recordset using one or more fields as sort keys. For example, you may want to view the recordset with the largest current balances displayed first. You sort recordsets by setting the sort box to Ascending or Descending for one or more fields in the Design grid. If you set the sort box for more than one field, the first field is used as the primary sort key, followed by the next field, and so on.

In this exercise, you will sort the results of the recordset you created in the last exercise.

1. Notice that the records in the recordset do not appear to be sorted in any particular order. *Actually, the records are sorted on the Customer ID field, which is the primary key for the Customers table. In the next few steps, you will set the sort key for the Lastname field in the Design grid. When you run the query again the recordset will be sorted by last name with the Jones record first, followed by the Roth record, and so on.*

2. Click the Design [icon] view button on the left end of the Access toolbar. *The Design grid will reappear. You can always use the Design view button to switch back and forth between the recordset and the Design grid.*

3. Follow these steps to set a sort key:

Field:	Firstname	Lastname	Phone	Current Balance
Table:	Customers	Customers	Customers	Customers
Sort:				
Show:	☑	Ascending	☑	☑
Criteria:		Descending		
or:		(not sorted)		

Ⓐ **Click in the Sort box for the Lastname field.**

Ⓑ **Click the drop-down button and choose Ascending from the list. The word Ascending will appear in the Sort box.**

4. Click the Run [icon] button and the following recordset will appear. *Notice that the records are sorted by the Lastname field.*

	FirstName	LastName	Phone	Current Balance
	Jason	Jones	(415) 312-2312	$48.00
	Mark	Roth	(510) 234-9090	$235.00
	Jacob	Samuels	(404) 367-8002	$250.50
	Tony	Simpson	(510) 238-2233	$185.00

5. Click the Design [icon] view button to display the Design grid.

6. Follow these steps to remove the Lastname sort key and to set the sort order to descending based on the Current Balance field:

Ⓐ **Click in the Sort box for the Lastname field.**

Ⓑ **Click the drop-down button and choose (not sorted). The Sort box will be cleared.**

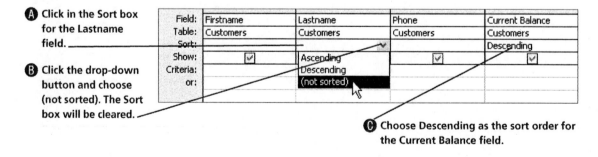

Field:	Firstname	Lastname	Phone	Current Balance
Table:	Customers	Customers	Customers	Customers
Sort:				Descending
Show:	☑	Ascending	☑	☑
Criteria:		Descending		
or:		(not sorted)		

Ⓒ **Choose Descending as the sort order for the Current Balance field.**

7. Click the Run ⚠ button and the following recordset will appear.
Notice that the records with the largest Current Balance are displayed first.

	FirstName	LastName	Phone	Current Balance
	Jacob	Samuels	(404) 367-8002	$250.50
	Mark	Roth	(510) 234-9090	$235.00
	Tony	Simpson	(510) 238-2233	$185.00
	Jason	Jones	(415) 312-2312	$48.00

8. Choose File→Close from the menu bar and click the Yes button when Access asks if you want to save the query.

9. Type the name **Sorted Customer Balance** in the Save As box and click OK.

Sorting with Multiple Fields

Access can sort on more than one field at a time. Queries evaluate the sort fields from left to right. If you add more than one sort to a query, Access will run a primary sort on the leftmost field in the Design grid and then run a secondary sort on the next field requested to the right.

 Hands-On 4.6   Sort with Multiple Fields

In this exercise, you will sort the Pets table on multiple fields.

1. Double-click the Create Query in Design View option.

2. Choose Pets from the Show Table box and click the Add button.

3. Click the Close button on the Show Table dialog box.

4. Resize the Query Design window to maximize your view of the Design grid and the Pets field list. You used this technique in Hands-On 4.1 with the Customers field list.

5. Add the Pet Name, Pet Type, and Expenditures fields to the Design grid.

6. Follow these steps to sort the Pet Type field in ascending order and the Expenditures field in descending order:

Ⓐ Click the Sort box for the Pet Type field.

Field:	Pet Name	Pet Type	Expenditures
Table:	Pets	Pets	Pets
Sort:		Ascending	Descending
Show:	✓	Ascending	✓
Criteria:		Descending	
or:		(not sorted)	

Ⓑ Click the drop-down button and choose Ascending as the sort order.

Ⓒ Click the Sort box for the Expenditures field then click the drop-down button and choose Descending.

7. Click the Run [!] button and the following recordset will appear.

Notice that the records are sorted first by Pet Type. Within the Pet Type, the records are sorted by Expenditures from largest to smallest amount.

Pet Name	Pet Type	Expenditures
Max	Cat	$1,450.55
Stripes	Cat	$450.00
Tony	Cat	$145.00
Spike	Dog	$890.00
Ben	Dog	$480.00
Wolfy	Dog	$450.00
Fetch	Dog	$345.00
Dillon	Dog	$150.55
Bugs	Rabbit	$600.50

8. Close the query and click Yes to save. Type **Pet Type Expenditures** in the Save As box.

Using Criteria to Select Records

One of the most important benefits of queries is that you can select specific records by specifying criteria. This gives you the ability to select the precise data you desire from a database. For example, you may want to know how many customers have an outstanding balance greater than $200. Or, perhaps you are interested in viewing only those records where the state is equal to CA. These and other questions are easily answered by specifying criteria in the Query Design grid.

Working with Equality Criteria

You can use equality criteria to choose only those records where a field has a specific value, such as CA. You accomplish this by entering the value you want the field to equal in the Criteria row of the Design grid. The following illustration shows how this is accomplished.

A This is a Criteria row.

Field:	FirstName	LastName	Phone	Current Balance	State
Table:	Customers	Customers	Customers	Customers	Customers
Sort:				Descending	
Show:	✓	✓	✓	✓	✓
Criteria:					CA
or:					

B Entering CA in the State Criteria box instructs Access to select only those records where the state is CA.

C As expected, only records where the state is CA appear in the recordset.

FirstName	LastName	Phone	Current Balance	State
Mark	Roth	(510) 234-9090	$235.00	CA
Tony	Simpson	(510) 238-2233	$185.00	CA
Jason	Jones	(415) 312-2312	$48.00	CA

Working with Comparison Criteria

You can use the comparison operators > (greater than), < (less than), >= (greater than or equal), <= (less than or equal), and NOT (not equal) when specifying criteria. Access will select only those records matching the criteria. For example, placing the criterion >200 in the Current Balance field instructs Access to select only records where the Current Balance is greater than 200.

The Show Check Box

The Show row in the Design grid contains a check box ☑ for each field. You can prevent a field from displaying in the recordset by removing the check from the Show box. This can be useful in many situations. For example, in the preceding illustration, the State field is used to select only records where the state is equal to CA. The State field must be present in the Design grid in order to specify these criteria. However, you may not want the State field to be displayed in the recordset. You can prevent the State field from being displayed by removing the check from the State field in the Design grid.

Hands-On 4.7   Use Criteria

In this exercise, you will experiment with equality and comparison criteria.

1. Double-click the Create Query in Design View option.

2. Choose Customers from the Show Table box and click the Add button.

3. Click the Close button on the Show Table dialog box.

4. Resize the Query Design window to maximize your view of the Design grid and the Pets field list.

5. Add the Firstname, Lastname, Phone, Current Balance, and State fields to the Design grid.

Use an Equality Criterion

6. Follow these steps to set an equality criterion for the State field:

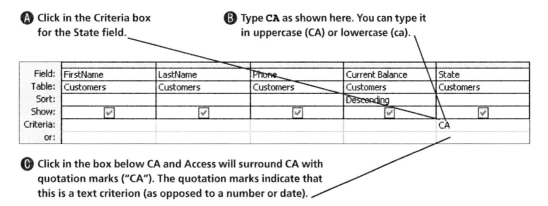

A Click in the Criteria box for the State field.

B Type **CA** as shown here. You can type it in uppercase (CA) or lowercase (ca).

Field:	FirstName	LastName	Phone	Current Balance	State
Table:	Customers	Customers	Customers	Customers	Customers
Sort:				Descending	
Show:	☑	☑	☑	☑	☑
Criteria:					CA
or:					

C Click in the box below CA and Access will surround CA with quotation marks ("CA"). The quotation marks indicate that this is a text criterion (as opposed to a number or date).

7. Click the Run [!] button.
   The three records with the State field equal to CA should appear in the recordset.

8. Click the Design [⊿] view button to display the Design grid.

Use Comparison Criteria

9. Follow these steps to create a "greater than" comparison criterion for the Current Balance field:

Field:	FirstName	LastName	Phone	Current Balance	State
Table:	Customers	Customers	Customers	Customers	Customers
Sort:					
Show:	☑	☑	☑	☑	☑
Criteria:				>200	

Ⓐ Click in the Criteria box for the Current Balance field and type **>200**.

Ⓑ Click in the Criteria box for the State field and delete the "CA" criterion.

10. Click the Run [!] button to produce the following recordset.
    Notice that the current balance is greater than $200 for each record.

FirstName	LastName	Phone	Current Balance	State
Mark	Roth	(510) 234-9090	$235.00	CA
Jacob	Samuels	(404) 367-8002	$250.50	GA

11. Click the Design [⊿] view button again to display the Design grid.

12. Change the >200 criterion to **<200** and run the query again.
    Only records with current balances less than $200 will appear in the recordset.

Uncheck the Show Box

In the next few steps, you will prevent the State field from appearing in the recordset by removing the check from the Show box.

13. Click the Design [⊿] view button to display the Design grid.

14. Follow these steps to set up the query:

Field:	FirstName	LastName	Phone	Current Balance	State
Table:	Customers	Customers	Customers	Customers	Customers
Sort:					
Show:	☑	☑	☑	☑	☐
Criteria:				<200	

Ⓐ Make sure the Current Balance criterion is set to <200.

Ⓑ Click the Show checkbox for the State field to remove the checkmark.

15. Click the Run ▣ button and the State field will be removed from the recordset.

16. Take 10 minutes to experiment with the query you have been using. Try entering various criteria and perhaps adding and removing fields from the Design grid. When you have finished experimenting, continue with the next topic.

Clearing the Design Grid

You can clear all entries from the Design grid with the Edit→Clear Grid command. This command can be used to give you a fresh start when working in the Design grid.

 Hands-On 4.8   **Clear the Grid and Add All Fields**

In this exercise, you will clear the Design grid to get a clean slate. Then you will add all fields from the Customers table into the Design grid.

1. If necessary, click the Design ▣ view button to display the Design grid.

2. Choose Edit→Clear Grid to remove all fields from the grid.

3. Follow these steps to add all fields from the Customers table to the Design grid:

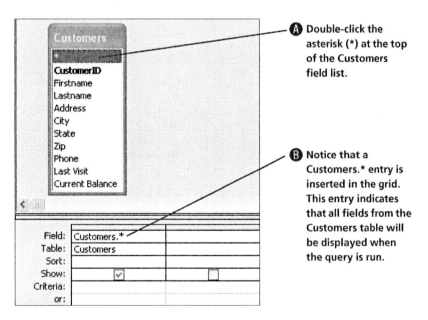

Ⓐ Double-click the asterisk (*) at the top of the Customers field list.

Ⓑ Notice that a Customers.* entry is inserted in the grid. This entry indicates that all fields from the Customers table will be displayed when the query is run.

4. Click the Run ▣ button. All records from the Customers table should appear in the recordset.

Use a Criterion to Select the Records

In the next few steps, you will add the Current Balance field to the Design grid and specify a criterion for that field.

5. Click the Design ![button] view button to display the Design grid.

6. Follow these steps to add the Current Balance field to the grid and to specify a criterion:

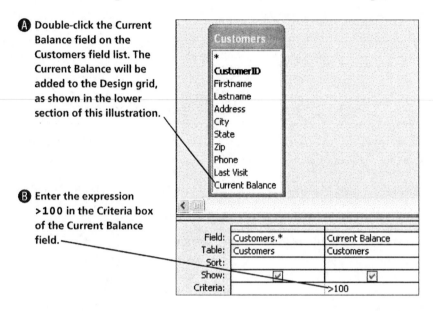

A Double-click the Current Balance field on the Customers field list. The Current Balance will be added to the Design grid, as shown in the lower section of this illustration.

B Enter the expression **>100** in the Criteria box of the Current Balance field.

7. Run ![button] the query to produce the recordset shown in the following illustration.

Customer ID	Firstname	Lastname	Address	City	State	Zip	Phone	Last Visit	Customers.Currer	Field0
1	Mark	Roth	760 Maple Avenue	Fremont	CA	94538-	(510) 234-9090	7/7/2003	$235.00	$235.00
2	Tony	Simpson	312 York Lane	Richmond	CA	94804-	(510) 238-2233	9/7/2003	$185.00	$185.00
4	Jacob	Samuels	2300 North Pratt Stre	Atlanta	GA	30309-	(404) 367-8002	10/8/2003	$250.50	$250.50

Notice that the last two columns of the recordset contain a Customers.Current Balance field and a Field0 field. This unusual nomenclature was used because the Current Balance field was included twice in the Query Design grid. It was included once as part of the Customers.* entry and again as a separate field in the second column. Access cannot display the same field name twice in a table or recordset; therefore, Access changed the names of the column headings in the recordset. You will correct this by removing the check from the Show box in the next few steps.

8. Switch to Design ![button] view and remove the check from the Show box of the Current Balance field. The Design grid should match the example shown to the right.

Field:	Customers.*	Current Balance
Table:	Customers	Customers
Sort:		
Show:	☑	☐
Criteria:		>100

9. Run the query. Notice that only one Current Balance field is visible.
The >100 criterion in the Current Balance field selects the appropriate records. However, the field is not displayed in the recordset because the Show box is unchecked.

10. Choose File→Close from the menu bar and click the Yes button to save the query.

11. Type the name **Current Balance** in the Save As box and click OK.

Using Wildcards in Queries

Wildcards are used in queries to find records where a field contains certain values. For example, you may want to display all records where the customer's name begins with the letter J. You can also use wildcards for numeric values. You may want to find the records of all customers who visited the clinic any day in the month of October.

 Hands-On 4.9 **Use Wildcards**

In this exercise, you will create a wildcard query for the Pet ID criteria.

1. Make sure the queries are displayed in the Database window.

2. Double-click the Create Query in Design View option.

3. Double-click Pets in the Show Table box then click the Close button.

4. Adjust the size of the Design grid and the Pets field list to so you can see the entire content of the field list.

5. Double-click the Pet ID, Pet Name, Pet Type, Color, and Last Visit fields to add those fields to the Design grid.

6. Follow these steps to add a wildcard to the criteria for Pet ID:

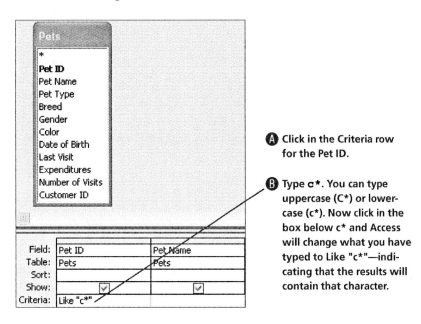

Ⓐ Click in the Criteria row for the Pet ID.

Ⓑ Type **c***. You can type uppercase (C*) or lowercase (c*). Now click in the box below c* and Access will change what you have typed to Like "c*"—indicating that the results will contain that character.

7. Click the Run [!] button to produce the recordset.
All records shown should have a Pet ID beginning with the letter C.

8. Click the Design [ ] view button to display the Design grid.

9. Click the Criteria box for the Pet ID field and delete the Like "c*" criterion.

10. Click in the Criteria box for Last Visit and type **7/*/2003**.

11. Click the Run ⊞ button to display the following recordset.

	Pet ID	Pet Name	Pet Type	Color	Last Visit
	CT92	Tony	Cat	Brown with black str	7/7/2003
	DG12	Wolfy	Dog	Brown	7/15/2003
	DG13	Dillon	Dog	Black	7/7/2003
	CT16	Stripes	Cat	Black and brown	7/15/2003

12. Choose File→Close from the menu bar and click the Yes button to save the query.

13. Type the name **July Visits** in the Save As box and click OK.

Working with Compound Criteria

Thus far, you have worked with relatively simple queries containing one criterion. However, you will sometimes need to use more than one criterion. Criteria composed of two or more criteria are known as compound criteria. There are two types of compound criteria: AND criteria and OR criteria.

AND Criteria

AND criteria let you select records based on logical AND expressions. In Hands-On 4.10, you will use AND criteria to select records in the Pets table. For example, you will use an AND expression to select all records where the pet type is dog and the number of visits is greater than 5. With AND criteria, Access will only select records when all of the criteria are true.

OR Criteria

OR criteria allow you to select records based on logical OR expressions. For example, you will use an OR expression to select all records where the pet type is dog or the pet type is cat. With OR criteria, Access will select records if any of the criteria are true.

Setting Up Compound Criteria

You set up compound criteria in the Design grid. AND criteria are set up by placing two or more criteria in different fields within the same Criteria row. OR criteria are set up by placing two or more criteria on different rows within the Design grid. The following illustration shows the compound criteria you will set up in Hands-On 4.10.

In this example, the criterion "dog" and >5 are on the same Criteria row. This creates an AND condition. Only records where the Pet Type is dog **and** the Number of Visits > 5 will be chosen.

Field:	Pet Name	Pet Type	Last Visit	Expenditures	Number of Visits
Table:	Pets	Pets	Pets	Pets	Pets
Sort:					
Show:	☑	☑	☑	☑	☑
Criteria:		"dog"			>5

In this example, the criteria are on different rows within the Pet Type field. This creates an OR condition as indicated by the Or heading at the left end of the second Criteria row. All records where the Pet Type is dog **or** the Pet Type is cat will be chosen.

Field:	Pet Name	Pet Type	Last Visit	Expenditures	Number of Visits
Table:	Pets	Pets	Pets	Pets	Pets
Sort:					
Show:	☑	☑	☑	☑	☑
Criteria:		"dog"			
or:		"cat"			

Hands-On 4.10   **Use Compound Criteria**

In this exercise, you will set up a new query using the Pets table from the Pinnacle Pet Care database. You will use compound criteria to query the database in various ways.

Set Up the Query Window

1. Make sure the queries are displayed in the Database window.
2. Double-click the Create Query in Design View option.
3. Choose Pets from the Show Table box and click the Add button.
4. Click the Close button on the Show Table dialog box.
5. Resize the Query Design window to maximize your view of the Design grid and the Pets field list.

Create an AND Criterion

6. Double-click the Pet Name, Pet Type, Last Visit, Expenditures, and Number of Visits fields on the Pets field list to add those fields to the Design grid.
7. Enter the following criteria into the Pet Type and Number of Visits boxes in the Criteria row:

Field:	Pet Name	Pet Type	Last Visit	Expenditures	Number of Visits
Table:	Pets	Pets	Pets	Pets	Pets
Sort:					
Show:	☑	☑	☑	☑	☑
Criteria:		"dog"			>5

8. Click the Run ⚡ button to produce the following recordset.

	Pet Name	Pet Type	Last Visit	Expenditures	Number of Visits
	Spike	Dog	10/8/2003	$890.00	12
	Wolfy	Dog	7/15/2003	$450.00	7

Notice that each record has Dog as the Pet Type and that the Number of Visits is greater than 5.

Create an OR Criterion

9. Switch to Design view and remove the >5 criterion from the Number of Visits criteria box.

10. Add the **cat** criterion to the row below the dog criterion as shown in the following illustration. It isn't necessary to type the quotation marks, though. Access will add them when you click outside of the field after typing the criterion.

TIP! *When using OR criteria, you can use as many rows as necessary. Each row that you add creates one more condition in the OR expression.*

Field:	Pet Name	Pet Type	Last Visit	Expenditures	Number of Visits
Table:	Pets	Pets	Pets	Pets	Pets
Sort:					
Show:	☑	☑	☑	☑	☑
Criteria:		"dog"			
or:		"cat"			

11. Click the Run ⚡ button to produce the following recordset.

	Pet Name	Pet Type	Last Visit	Expenditures	Number of Visits
	Tony	Cat	7/7/2003	$145.00	6
	Ben	Dog	10/8/2003	$480.00	3
	Spike	Dog	10/8/2003	$890.00	12
	Wolfy	Dog	7/15/2003	$450.00	7
	Dillon	Dog	7/7/2003	$150.55	3
	Max	Cat	9/7/2003	$1,450.55	20
	Stripes	Cat	7/15/2003	$450.00	9
	Fetch	Dog	9/10/2003	$345.00	3

Notice that all records have a Pet Type of Dog or Cat.

Use a Combination of AND and OR Compound Criteria

12. Switch to Design ![icon] view but do not change the "dog" and "cat" criteria.

13. Add the **>5** criteria to the Number of Visits field, as shown in the following illustration.

Field:	Pet Name	Pet Type	Last Visit	Expenditures	Number of Visits
Table:	Pets	Pets	Pets	Pets	Pets
Sort:					
Show:	☑	☑	☑	☑	☑
Criteria:		"dog"			>5
or:		"cat"			>5

These compound criteria will choose all records where the Pet Type is Dog and the Number of Visits is greater than 5 or the Pet Type is Cat and the Number of Visits is greater than 5.

14. Click the Run ![icon] button to produce the following recordset.

Pet Name	Pet Type	Last Visit	Expenditures	Number of Visits
Tony	Cat	7/7/2003	$145.00	6
Spike	Dog	10/8/2003	$890.00	12
Wolfy	Dog	7/15/2003	$450.00	7
Max	Cat	9/7/2003	$1,450.55	20
Stripes	Cat	7/15/2003	$450.00	9

15. Switch to Design view and take 10 minutes to experiment with compound criteria.
Be creative! Query the Pets table for answers to any questions that may come to mind.

16. When you have finished experimenting, choose File→Close from the menu bar and click the Yes button when Access asks if you want to save the query.

17. Type the name **Compound Criteria** in the Save As box and click OK.

Formatting and Printing Query Results

Although reports are often used to print query results, recordsets can be formatted and printed just like you printed datasheets in Lesson 1, Creating Tables and Entering Data. In Hands-On 4.11 you will format and print the results of a query.

In this exercise, you will format the Current Balance query then print it.

1. Make sure the Query button is selected in the Objects bar.

2. Double-click the Sorted Customer Balance query to run the query and display the recordset.

3. If necessary open the formatting toolbar by choosing View→Toolbars→Formatting (Datasheet).

4. Follow these steps to format the recordset for printing:

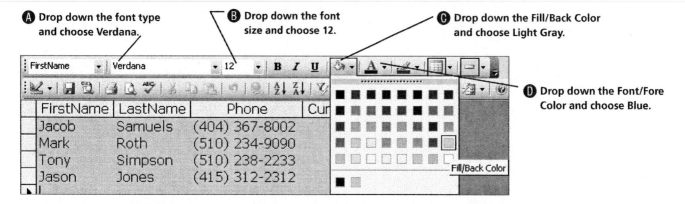

Ⓐ Drop down the font type and choose Verdana.

Ⓑ Drop down the font size and choose 12.

Ⓒ Drop down the Fill/Back Color and choose Light Gray.

Ⓓ Drop down the Font/Fore Color and choose Blue.

5. Position your mouse pointer on the FirstName field, press and hold down the left mouse button, and drag the mouse over all four column headings to select them.

6. Choose Format→Column Width from the menu and click the Best Fit button.

7. Click the Print Preview 🔍 button on the Access toolbar.
   The Print Preview window should display the following recordset.

	Sorted Customer Balance		11/17/2003
FirstName	LastName	Phone	Current Balance
Jacob	Samuels	(404) 367-8002	$250.50
Mark	Roth	(510) 234-9090	$235.00
Tony	Simpson	(510) 238-2233	$185.00
Jason	Jones	(415) 312-2312	$48.00

8. Print the query results and close the query.

9. Click the Yes button when Access asks if you want to save the changes.

10. Close the Pinnacle Pet Care database and continue with the end-of-lesson questions and exercises.

 # Concepts Review

True/False Questions

1. Criteria determine the records selected by a query.   TRUE   FALSE

2. The Query Design grid is where you define a query.   TRUE   FALSE

3. You can add fields to the Design grid by double-clicking the desired fields on the   TRUE   FALSE
   field list(s) above the Design grid.

4. You can add all fields to the Design grid by double-clicking any field in the   TRUE   FALSE
   field list.

5. Changing data in the recordset has no impact on the underlying data in the   TRUE   FALSE
   table(s) on which the query is based.

6. You must type criteria in the same case (uppercase or lowercase) as the data in the   TRUE   FALSE
   tables you are querying or Access will not select the desired records.

7. If a field has been entered into the Design grid, you cannot prevent the field from   TRUE   FALSE
   appearing in the recordset.

8. The two types of compound criteria are AND and OR.   TRUE   FALSE

9. You cannot use wildcards for numeric values.   TRUE   FALSE

10. Access can sort on more than one field at a time.   TRUE   FALSE

Multiple Choice Questions

1. Which of the following commands can be
   used to remove fields from the Design grid?
   a. Field→Remove
   b. Edit→Delete Columns
   c. Edit→Delete Rows
   d. File→Delete Columns

2. Which of the following symbols is used to
   represent greater than in query criteria?
   a. <
   b. >
   c. <=
   d. >=

3. Which of the following commands is used
   to clear the Design grid?
   a. File→Clear All
   b. File→Clear Grid
   c. Edit→Clear Grid
   d. The grid cannot be cleared.

4. Which symbol(s) can be used as a Wildcard
   in query criteria?
   a. !
   b. *
   c. (
   d. &

Skill Builders

Skill Builder 4.1   Use Compound Criteria

In this exercise, you will use compound criteria to query the Customers table in the Tropical Getaways database.

1. Open the Tropical Getaways database and click the Queries button on the Objects bar.

2. Double-click the Create Query in Design view option.

3. Choose Customers in the Show Table box and click the Add button.

4. Click the Close button to close the Show Table dialog box.

5. If necessary, maximize the Query window. Adjust the height of the Design grid and the Customers field list box.

6. Add the Firstname, Lastname, and Profile fields to the Design grid by double-clicking them on the Customers field list.

7. Type the word **adventure** in the Criteria box of the Profile field, as shown here.

Field:	Firstname	Lastname	Profile
Table:	Customers	Customers	Customers
Sort:			
Show:	☑	☑	☑
Criteria:			adventure

8. Run ![run] the query. Only records with the Adventure profile will be displayed, as shown here.

Firstname	Lastname	Profile
Debbie	Thomas	Adventure
Ted	Wilkins	Adventure
Victor	Thomas	Adventure

9. Switch back to Design ![design] view.

10. Add the State field to the Design grid.

11. Set the criteria for the State field to **TX** and the sort order of the Lastname field to Ascending, as shown in the following figure.

Field:	Firstname	Lastname	Profile	State
Table:	Customers	Customers	Customers	Customers
Sort:		Ascending		
Show:	☑	☑	☑	☑
Criteria:			"adventure"	TX

12. Run the query. Only records where the profile is Adventure and the state is TX will be displayed, as shown in the following figure.

	Firstname	Lastname	Profile	State
	Debbie	Thomas	Adventure	TX
	Ted	Wilkins	Adventure	TX

13. Close the query and save it as **Adventure Profiles**.

Skill Builder 4.2   Use Comparison Criteria

In this exercise, you will use comparison criteria to query the Trips table in the Tropical Getaways database.

1. Double-click the Create Query in Design view option.

2. Choose Trips in the Show Table box and click the Add button.

3. Click the Close button to close the Show Table dialog box.

4. If necessary, maximize the Query window. Adjust the height of the Design grid and the Trips field list box.

5. Add the Destination, Category, and Cost fields to the Design grid by double-clicking on them.

6. Click in the criteria row in the Cost field and type **<3000**, as shown in the following figure.

Field:	Destination	Category	Cost
Table:	Trips	Trips	Trips
Sort:			
Show:	✓	✓	✓
Criteria:			<3000

7. Click the Run [ ] button. Only records where the cost is below $3,000 will be displayed, as shown here.

	Destination	Category	Cost
	Caribbean Cruise	Leisure	$2,390.00
	Baja California	Adventu	$1,750.00
	Rocky Mountains	Adventu	$2,190.00
	Baja California	Adventu	$2,900.00

8. Close the query and save it as **Trips Under $3000**.

Skill Builder 4.3   Use Wildcards and Sort Records

In this exercise, you will use wildcards in the criteria and sort records in the Trips table.

1. Double-click the Create Query in Design view option.

2. Choose Trips in the Show Table box and click the Add button.

3. Click the Close button to close the Show Table dialog box.

4. If necessary, maximize the Query window. Adjust the height of the Design grid and the Trips field list box.

5. Add the Trip ID, Destination, Category, and Departure Date fields to the Design grid by double-clicking them on the Trips field list.

6. Type **8/*/2004** in the Criteria box of the Departure date field. When you click in another box, Access will change what you have typed to Like "8/*/2004".

7. Click on the sort row of the Destination field and set the sort order to Ascending, as shown in the following figure.

Field:	Trip ID	Destination	Category	Departure Date
Table:	Trips	Trips	Trips	Trips
Sort:		Ascending		
Show:	☑	☑	☑	☑
Criteria:				Like "8/*/2004"

8. Run 🔲 the query. Only records where the date is in the month of August will be displayed, as shown in the following figure.

	Trip ID	Destination	Category	Departure Date
	Adv02	Amazon Jungle Trek	Adventu	8/7/2004
	Adv06	Baja California	Adventu	8/8/2004
	Adv01	Kenyan Safari	Adventu	8/5/2004

9. Close the query and save it as **August Departures**.

10. Close the Tropical Getaways database.

Assessments

Assessment 4.1   Create Queries

In this exercise, you will create a new query to the Classic Cars database.

1. Open the Classic Cars database.

2. Create a new query and add the Collectors table to it.

3. Set up the query to produce the recordset shown in the following illustration. Notice that this query simply chooses the indicated fields and sorts the records in descending order by Collection Size.

Firstname	Lastname	Era of Interest	Collection Size
Cindy	Johnson	1950's	42
Ed	Larkson	Early 1900's	34
Angela	Hall	1960's	12
Bob	Barker	1950's	7
Isaac	Williams	1940's	6
Tammy	Olson	1960's	6
Jake	Johnson	1920's	3
Anthony	Jeffers	1930's	3

4. Run the query and print the recordset. Now close the query and save it as **Collection Sizes**.

5. Create a new query and add the Cars table to it.

6. Set up the query to produce the recordset shown in the following illustration. (You'll run and format the recordset in a moment). Notice that this query only selects records where the model is Corvette and the condition is Excellent. The query also sorts the records by Value, with the largest values appearing first.

7. Run the query, format the recordset by changing the font to Verdana, the font size to 12pt, the text color to Dark Blue, and the background to Light Gray.

8. Autofit the width of all columns to fit the largest entry/heading in the columns.

Make	Model	Year	Color	Condition	Value
Chevrolet	Corvette	57	Red	Excellent	$42,000.00
Chevrolet	Corvette	58	Black	Excellent	$35,000.00
Chevrolet	Corvette	62	Blue	Excellent	$30,000.00

9. Print the recordset. Now close the query and save it as **Excellent Corvettes**.

Assessment 4.2 · **Create Queries**

In this exercise, you will create queries with compound criteria and that are sorted in specific orders.

1. Create a new query and add the Cars table to it.

2. Set up the query to produce the following recordset. Notice that the query selects records where the make is Chevrolet and the Value is under $40,000.

Make	Model	Condition	Value
Chevrolet	Corvette	Excellent	$30,000.00
Chevrolet	Corvette	Excellent	$35,000.00
Chevrolet	Camaro	Mint	$27,500.00

3. Run the query and print the recordset. Now close the query and save it as **Chevrolets Under $40000**.

4. Create a new query and add the Cars table to the Query Design grid.

5. Set up the query to produce the following recordset. Notice that this query only selects records where the year begins with a 5 and is sorted by Make in Alphabetical order.

Car ID	Year	Make	Model
BB04	57	Chevrolet	Corvette
BB03	58	Chevrolet	Corvette
CJ01	58	Chevrolet	Corvette
CJ22	59	Ford	Thunderbird

6. Run the query and print the recordset. Now close the query and save it as **50s Cars**.

7. Close the Classic Cars database when you have finished then exit from Access.

# Critical Thinking

Critical Thinking 4.1   Create Select Queries

Linda Holmes has created an add-on service for investor contacts only. She has asked you to create a select query that chooses only the records from the Contacts table in which the contact type is Investor. Open the Holmestead Realty database and follow these guidelines to create a select query:

- The recordset should display only the Firstname, Lastname, Spousename, Phone, and Contact Type fields from the Contacts table.

- Only contacts with a contact type of Investor should appear in the recordset.

- Save the query as **Investors**.

Linda has published a brochure that she sends only to contacts who have a contact type of Primary Resident or Trustee. Follow these guidelines to set up a select query:

- The recordset should display only the Firstname, Lastname, Address, City, State, Zip, and Contact Type fields from the Contacts table.

- Only contacts with a contact type of Primary Residence or Trustee should appear in the recordset.

- Save the query as **Non-Investors**.

Critical Thinking 4.2   Create Queries

Linda has a customer who would like to purchase a duplex under $200,000. She has asked you to create a query that shows only those records.

- The recordset should display only the MLS#, Street#, Address, Price, and Style fields.

- Only listings with the style of duplex and a price under $200,000 should appear in the recordset.

- Save the query as **Duplexes Under $200000**.

Linda would like to increase the advertising on the listings that will expire in the next month. She would like you to create a query that lists the listings that will expire in the month of January.

- The recordset should display only the MLS#, Seller ID, and Expiration Date.

- Only listings that have a date that begins with 01 should appear in the recordset.

- Save the query as **Listings Expiring in January**.

- Save the changes to Holmestead Realty database, close it, and exit from Access.

Creating Advanced Queries

In this lesson, you will set up and use advanced queries. You will often have more than one table in a database. Relationships are set up to tie tables together whenever possible. Often you will need to extract data from more than one table and tie the information. For instance, in the Pinnacle Pet Care database, you have a Customers table and a Pets table. These tables are related in that the customers have pets and the pets belong to the customers. The common field in both tables is Customer ID.

Using the Customer ID, you can run a query that shows the pet information and the owner's address or phone number. In this lesson, you will learn how to set up a variety of queries that select data from multiple tables. You will create calculated fields, work with statistical functions, and sort and group query results. You will also set up parameter queries that prompt users to enter a criteria range and action queries that modify tables. Any of these queries can be used as the basis for reports.

Microsoft Office Access 2003 objectives covered in this lesson

Objective Number	Skill Sets and Skills	Concept Page References	Exercise Page References
AC03S-1-5	Create and modify one-to-many relationships	118	119–120, 141–142
AC03S-1-6	Enforce referential integrity	119	121
AC03S-1-7	Create and modify queries	133–134	130–131, 133–135, 151–153
AC03S-1-10	Create reports		147–148
AC03S-3-1	Create and modify calculated fields and aggregate functions	123–124, 127	124–125, 127–128, 143–145, 149

Additional learning resources are available at **labpub.com/learn/access03/**

Case Study

The office staff at Pinnacle Pet Care is excited about the information they can retrieve with queries. They have asked Al Smith to include more queries. They would like to see:

- Total expenditures for each pet

- Average amount spent on cats and dogs

They would also like to be able to run reports showing pets overdue for visits so the office staff can contact the owners.

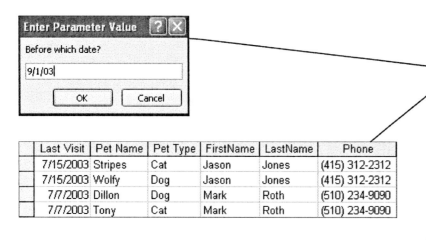

A parameter query creates a pop-up box that requires you to enter a criterion. This one asks for a date. This date is placed in the criteria of the query as <9/1/03. The query runs and produces this recordset. This recordset is used as the dataset for this report.

Last Visit	Pet Name	Pet Type	FirstName	LastName	Phone
7/15/2003	Stripes	Cat	Jason	Jones	(415) 312-2312
7/15/2003	Wolfy	Dog	Jason	Jones	(415) 312-2312
7/7/2003	Dillon	Dog	Mark	Roth	(510) 234-9090
7/7/2003	Tony	Cat	Mark	Roth	(510) 234-9090

Overdue for Visit

Last Visit	Pet Name	Pet Type	FirstName	LastName	Phone
7/7/2003	Dillon	Dog	Mark	Roth	(510) 234-9090
7/7/2003	Tony	Cat	Mark	Roth	(510) 234-9090
7/15/2003	Stripes	Cat	Jason	Jones	(415) 312-2312
7/15/2003	Wolfy	Dog	Jason	Jones	(415) 312-2312

Working with Relationships

In a properly designed Access database, different types of data are stored in separate tables. For example, all customer data is stored in a Customers table and all pet data is stored in the Pets table. Storing data in separate tables is essential if you want to create a clean and flexible database system. However, it is also important to have a mechanism that allows you to "bring the data back together." For example, suppose you need to create a report that displays data from both the Customers and Pets tables. To accomplish this, you must create a relationship between the tables. Relationships determine how the records in one table are related to the records in another table. For example, each pet in the Pinnacle Pet Care database is owned by or related to a customer in the Customers table.

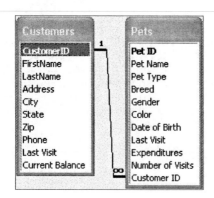

The relationship between the Customers and Pets tables is established through the Customer ID field, which appears in both tables. Each customer can have many pets. Thus, a one-to-many relationship will be established between the tables.

Establishing Table Relationships

You create relationships between tables by matching key fields in the tables. The key fields are typically the primary key in one table and a foreign key in the other table. The key fields typically have the same name, and they must have the same data type. For example, the relationship used in the preceding illustration matches the Customer ID field in the Customers table with the Customer ID field in the Pets table. The Customer ID field determines the relationship between the two tables. The primary purpose of the relationship is to synchronize the records. For example, imagine you create a report that lists each pet in the database along with the pet owner. The relationship between the Customer ID fields in both tables will ensure that the proper customer is displayed for each pet.

One-to-Many Relationships

A one-to-many relationship is common. When you define a relationship, the one-to-many is the default type. It exists between two tables when one record in a primary table relates to many records in the secondary table. For instance, one customer can have many pets but each pet can only have one customer related to it.

Many-to-Many Relationships

A many-to-many relationship exists when more than two tables are involved. The relationship is defined between a primary table, a secondary table, and a junction table. The junction table contains fields that are the primary keys in the primary and secondary tables. For instance, we have three tables: a Customers table, a Pets table, and a Visits table. Any one customer can have many pets and can have many visits to the clinic.

Enforcing Referential Integrity

When you create a relationship, Access gives you the option of enforcing referential integrity between the tables. Referential integrity prevents you from using a value in the foreign key of one table unless the same value exists as a primary key in the other table. For example, in the Pinnacle Pet Care database, referential integrity will allow you to enter a Customer ID in the Pets table only if that Customer ID is used in the Customers table. In other words, referential integrity ensures that every pet is associated with a customer. Referential integrity also prevents you from deleting a customer record from the Customers table if a record in the Pets table uses that Customer ID.

QUICK REFERENCE: ESTABLISHING RELATIONSHIPS

Task	Procedure
Establish a relationship between tables	■ Open the desired database and click the Relationships button or choose Tools→Relationships from the menu bar.
	■ Use the Show Table box to add the tables between which you wish to establish the relationship.
	■ Close the Show Table box.
	■ Drag the field that will be used to establish the relationship from the primary table to the field to which it will be linked in the secondary table.
	■ If desired, use the Join button to change the join, or relationship, type.
	■ If desired, use the Enforce Referential Integrity box to enforce referential integrity.
	■ Click the Create button to create the relationship.
	■ Close the Relationships window.

 Hands-On 5.1 ## Establish a Relationship and Enforce Referential Integrity

In this exercise, you will establish a relationship between the Customers and Pets tables in the Pinnacle Pet Care database.

1. Start Access and open the Pinnacle Pet Care database.

2. Click the Relationships [icon] button on the Access toolbar.
   The Relationships window will open and the Show Table box will appear.

3. Choose the Customers table and click the Add button.
   The Customers table will be added to the Relationships window.

4. Now add the Pets table to the Relationships window and close the Show Table box.

5. Follow these steps to adjust the size of the Customers and Pets field lists:

Ⓐ Position the mouse pointer on the bottom edge of the Customers field list and a double-headed arrow will appear.

Ⓑ Drag the bottom edge of the list down until all fields are visible.

Ⓒ Extend the Pets field list until all fields are visible.

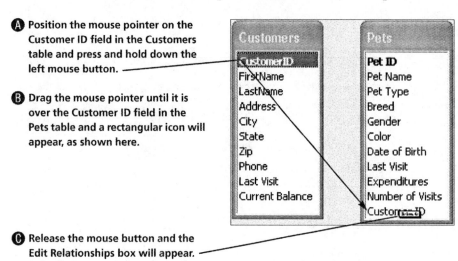

6. Follow these steps to establish a relationship between the Customer ID fields:

Ⓐ Position the mouse pointer on the Customer ID field in the Customers table and press and hold down the left mouse button.

Ⓑ Drag the mouse pointer until it is over the Customer ID field in the Pets table and a rectangular icon will appear, as shown here.

Ⓒ Release the mouse button and the Edit Relationships box will appear.

The Edit Relationships box lets you choose the desired relationship type. The default relationship type is one-to-many.

!TIP! *If you have any trouble establishing a relationship, go back to your table design and make sure the fields you are using have the same data type.*

7. Follow these steps to enforce referential integrity and to examine the options in the Edit Relationships box:

Ⓐ Check this box to enforce referential integrity.

Ⓑ Notice this checkbox (but don't check it). If the Cascade Update Related Fields box were checked, Access would automatically change the values in the Customer ID fields in the Pets table, but only if the corresponding Customer IDs were changed in the Customers table. If the box is unchecked, you cannot change Customer IDs in the Customers table.

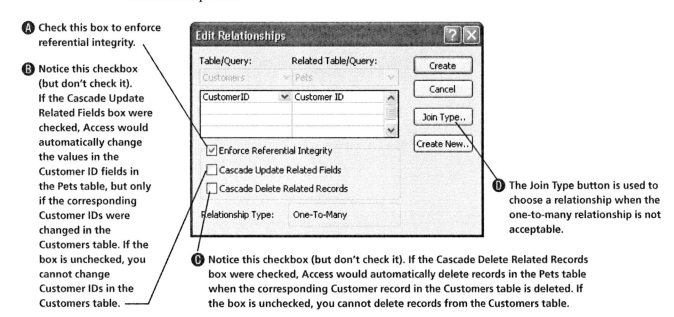

Ⓓ The Join Type button is used to choose a relationship when the one-to-many relationship is not acceptable.

Ⓒ Notice this checkbox (but don't check it). If the Cascade Delete Related Records box were checked, Access would automatically delete records in the Pets table when the corresponding Customer record in the Customers table is deleted. If the box is unchecked, you cannot delete records from the Customers table.

8. Click the Create button to complete the relationship.
A join line will connect the Customer ID fields in the tables.

9. Follow these steps to understand the relationship:

Ⓐ Notice that the Customer ID field in the Customers table is marked with a 1, indicating that this is the one side of the relationship. In other words, each Customer ID in the Customers table will only appear once in the Customers table.

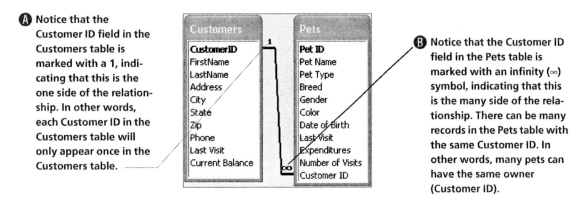

Ⓑ Notice that the Customer ID field in the Pets table is marked with an infinity (∞) symbol, indicating that this is the many side of the relationship. There can be many records in the Pets table with the same Customer ID. In other words, many pets can have the same owner (Customer ID).

The relationship is now established and can be used to help you develop queries, forms, and reports.

10. Leave the Relationships window open and continue with the next topic.

Modifying Relationships

 You can add tables and set relationships at any time, but they are most easily added after a relationship has been established. A table is added to the relationship window by clicking the Show Table button on the toolbar then double-clicking on the table you would like to add. Once the table is added, relationships can be established between it and the other tables in the relationship window.

Hands-On 5.2   Add Tables and Relationships

In this exercise, you will add a table and establish additional relationships between the Visits table and the Pets table.

1. Click the Show Table button.

2. Add the Visits table and close the Show Table box.
   If you accidentally add a table twice, click the title bar of the extra table and press the Delete *key on the keyboard.*

3. Drag the bottom edge of the field list down until all fields are visible.

4. Position the mouse pointer over the Pet ID field on the Pets list.

5. Press the left mouse button and drag until the Pet ID field is over the Pet ID field in the Visits list.
   The Relationships window will open.

6. Check the Enforce Referential Integrity box.

7. Click the Create button to complete the relationship.
   Your relationship window should match the following illustration.

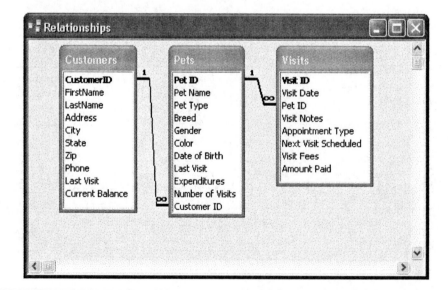

Printing Relationships

The File→Print Relationships command is available whenever the Relationships window is open. When you choose this command, Access prepares a report that displays the same relationships that are displayed in the Relationships window. You can then print the relationships by clicking the Print button on the Access toolbar.

 Hands-On 5.3 Print Relationships

In this exercise, you will print the relationship you created in Hands-On 5.2. The Relationships window should still be displayed.

1. Choose File→Print Relationships from the menu bar.
   Access will require a few moments to prepare the report.

2. If desired, click the Print ⊟ button on the toolbar to print the report.

3. Close the report window without saving the report.

4. Close the Relationships window and click Yes if Access asks you to save the changes.

Working with Advanced Queries

So far, you have worked with simple queries. Now we will look at Access' other, more complex queries. Calculated fields, statistical functions, parameter queries, crosstab queries, and action queries are among the more advanced query tools available.

Calculated Fields

Access lets you create calculated fields within queries. Calculated fields perform calculations using values from other fields within the query or from fields in the underlying table(s). For example, in Hands-On 5.4, you will set up a new query based on the Pets table. The Pets table contains an Expenditures field that represents the total expenditures for a particular pet. The Pets table also contains a Number of Visits field that represents the total number of visits by the pet. You will create a calculated field within the query named Expenditures Per Visit, which will be calculated as the Expenditures divided by the Number of Visits. The following illustration shows the Design grid with the Pet Name and Pet Type fields and the Expenditures Per Visit calculated field.

Field:	Pet Name	Pet Type	Expenditures Per Vis
Table:	Pets	Pets	
Sort:			
Show:	✓	✓	✓
Criteria:			

Expenditures Per Visit is a calculated field. It is too wide to be completely visible in the cell. The complete content of the cell is Expenditures Per Visit: [Expenditures]/ [Number of Visits].

The following illustration outlines the syntax that must be used with calculated fields.

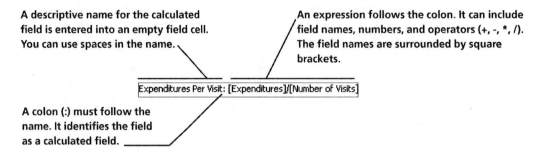

A descriptive name for the calculated field is entered into an empty field cell. You can use spaces in the name.

An expression follows the colon. It can include field names, numbers, and operators (+, -, *, /). The field names are surrounded by square brackets.

Expenditures Per Visit: [Expenditures]/[Number of Visits]

A colon (:) must follow the name. It identifies the field as a calculated field.

The Zoom Box

Calculated field expressions can be quite long and complex. For this reason, you may not be able to see the entire expression as you enter it in a cell. Fortunately, Access provides a Zoom command that displays a Zoom box. When you enter the desired expression into the Zoom box, you can see the entire expression as it is entered. In Hands-On 5.4, you will use the Zoom box to enter an expression. You display the Zoom box by right-clicking the cell where the expression will be entered and choosing Zoom from the pop-up menu.

 Hands-On 5.4   Create a Calculated Field

In this exercise, you will set up a query with a calculated field.

1. Click the Queries button on the Objects bar.

2. Create a new query in Design view and add the Pets table to it.

3. Close the Show Tables dialog box.

4. Add the Pet Name and Pet Type fields to the Design grid.

5. Follow these steps to display the Zoom box:

A Click in the empty field cell to the right of Pet Type.

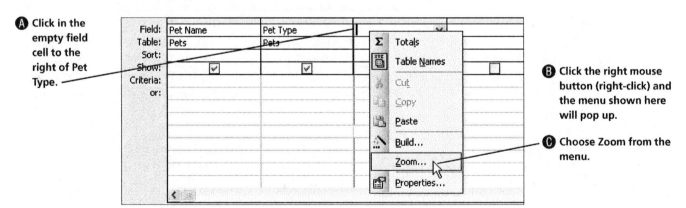

B Click the right mouse button (right-click) and the menu shown here will pop up.

C Choose Zoom from the menu.

6. Enter the calculated field expression shown in the following illustration into the Zoom box.

Make sure you enter the expression exactly as shown. In particular, make sure you use a colon (:) and not a semicolon (;), correctly spell the field names, use the correct open and closed brackets [ ], and use the forward slash (/) to represent division. Access is lenient when it comes to spaces, so you can omit the spaces that come after the colon and before and after the forward slash if you desire. Access is not lenient when it comes to the spelling of field names. They must be spelled exactly as they appear in the field name—including spaces.

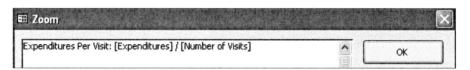

7. Click OK to insert the expression in the field.

8. Make sure the syntax is correct as shown in the preceding illustration. If necessary, you can edit the expression within the cell or redisplay the Zoom dialog box and make any necessary changes.

9. Click the Run ![run] button to produce the recordset shown to the right.

The numbers shown in the Expenditures Per Visit field represent the average expenditure for each pet on each visit. Notice the excessive number of decimal places that are displayed in the calculated field. In Hands-On 5.5, you will reduce the number of displayed decimal places by changing one of the properties of the Expenditures Per Visit field.

Pet Name	Pet Type	Expenditures P
Max	Cat	72.5275
Stripes	Cat	50
Tony	Cat	24.1666666667
Wolfy	Dog	64.2857142857
Dillon	Dog	50.1833333333
Fetch	Dog	115
Ben	Dog	160
Spike	Dog	74.1666666667
Bugs	Rabbit	150.125

10. Switch to Design ![design] view and continue with the next topic.

Modifying Query Properties

The Properties ![properties] button on the Access toolbar displays the Properties dialog box. You use this dialog box to change the properties of any Access object, including fields within queries. Properties can affect the appearance and format of objects. For example, in Hands-On 5.5, you will set the Format property of the Expenditures Per Visit calculated field to Currency. The Currency format will reduce the number of displayed decimal places in the recordset.

In this exercise, you will format the results of the calculation to show as currency. The Query Design grid should be displayed from the previous exercise.

1. Click in the Expenditures Per Visit box then click the Properties button on the toolbar. *The Field Properties dialog box will appear.*

2. Follow these steps to set the format of this field to Currency:

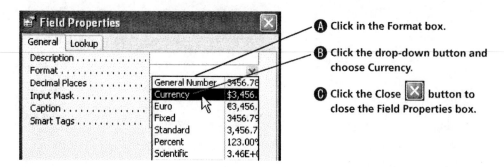

When the query is run, the Currency format will display a dollar sign and two decimal places in the Expenditures Per Visit field.

3. Click the Run ! button.
The numbers in the Expenditures Per Visit field should now be formatted with the Currency format. Note the dollar sign and two decimal places.

4. Switch to Design view.

Insert a Criterion

5. Click in the Criteria box for the Pet Type field and type **dog**.

Field:	Pet Name	Pet Type	Expenditures Per Vis
Table:	Pets	Pets	
Sort:			
Show:	☑	☑	☑
Criteria:		dog ◄	

6. Click the Run ! button.
Pet Name, Pet Type, and Expenditures Per Visit will be displayed for records where the Pet Type is Dog. As you can see, Access allows you to combine criteria, calculated fields, and other parameters within a query.

7. Choose File→Close to close the query and save it as **Expenditures Per Visit**.

Statistical Functions

Access provides built-in statistical functions for calculating statistical information within a query. The built-in statistical functions include Sum (summation), Avg (average), Min (minimum), Max (maximum), Count, Var (variance), First, and Last. Adding statistical functions is simple and can enhance your queries. For example, you can use the Avg function to compute the average expenditures on pets, or you can use the Count function to track the number of dogs that attend the Pinnacle Pet Care clinic.

The Total Row

To use the statistical functions, you must first click the Totals button to display a Total row in the Query Design grid. Once the Total row is displayed, you can choose statistical function(s) for the desired field(s) in the query. Queries that use statistical functions will sometimes have just one or two fields.

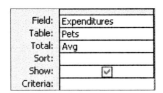

Statistical functions are entered in the Total row of the Query Design grid.

 Hands-On 5.6   Use Statistical Functions

In this exercise, you will use a statistical function to show the average of pet expenditures.

1. Set up a new query in Design view and add the Pets table to it.

2. Close the Show Tables dialog box.

3. Add the Expenditures field to the Design grid.

4. Click the Totals Σ button on the toolbar and a Total row will appear below the Table row.
   The Total row lets you choose statistical functions and set grouping for fields. You will learn about grouping in the Using Grouping with Statistical Functions section on page 129.

5. Follow these steps to choose the Avg function for the Expenditures field:
   When you run the query, Access will determine the average expenditure for all pets. Access will display a single cell in the recordset containing the result of the average calculation.

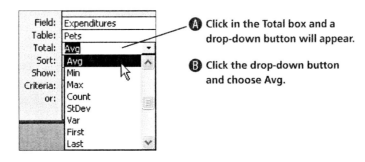

Ⓐ Click in the Total box and a drop-down button will appear.

Ⓑ Click the drop-down button and choose Avg.

6. Click the Run ![Run button] button.

   The result should be $551.29. In other words, each pet has been responsible for an average of $551.29 in revenue.

7. Switch to Design ![Design view] view and click in the Total box that currently contains the Avg function.

8. Click the drop-down button, scroll to the top of the list, and choose Sum.

9. Run ![Run button] the query again. This time the result should be $4,961.60.

   This number represents the summation of the expenditures for all pets.

10. Switch to Design ![Design view] view and continue with the next topic.

Using Criteria with Statistical Functions

You can combine criteria with statistical functions to refine your statistical calculations. For example, imagine you want to determine the total expenditures for dogs at Pinnacle Pet Care. The answer can be found by summing the expenditures of all records where the Pet Type is dog. The following illustration shows how this is expressed in the Design grid.

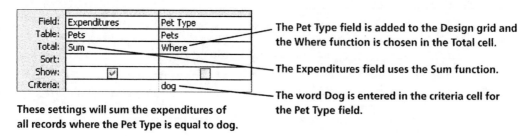

Field:	Expenditures	Pet Type
Table:	Pets	Pets
Total:	Sum	Where
Sort:		
Show:	☑	☐
Criteria:		dog

The Pet Type field is added to the Design grid and the Where function is chosen in the Total cell.

The Expenditures field uses the Sum function.

The word Dog is entered in the criteria cell for the Pet Type field.

These settings will sum the expenditures of all records where the Pet Type is equal to dog.

 Hands-On 5.7   Use Criteria with Statistical Functions

In this exercise, you will use a statistical function to show the average expenditures of just the dogs.

1. Double-click the Pet Type field on the Pets field list to add it to the Design grid.

2. Follow these steps to specify criteria for the Pet Type field:

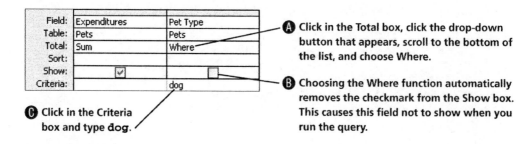

Field:	Expenditures	Pet Type
Table:	Pets	Pets
Total:	Sum	Where
Sort:		
Show:	☑	☐
Criteria:		dog

Ⓐ Click in the Total box, click the drop-down button that appears, scroll to the bottom of the list, and choose Where.

Ⓑ Choosing the Where function automatically removes the checkmark from the Show box. This causes this field not to show when you run the query.

Ⓒ Click in the Criteria box and type **dog**.

3. Run the query. The result should be $2,315.55.

   This number represents the total expenditures on dogs.

4. Switch back to Design view and continue with the next topic.

Using Grouping with Statistical Functions

The Total row in the Design grid has a Group By option that can be used in conjunction with statistical functions. If you choose Group By for a field and run the query, Access will group all records that have the same value in the Group By field. For example, if the Pet Type field is set to Group By, all records with Cat as the Pet Type will be in one group. Likewise, all records with a Pet Type of Dog will be in another group. If you are also performing a statistical calculation, it will be performed on each group. For example, if you use the Sum function to calculate the expenditures for the groups just mentioned, the total expenditures for cats will be calculated, as will the total expenditures for dogs.

 Hands-On 5.8   **Use the Group By Setting**

In this exercise, you will group the averages of pet expenditures by pet type.

1. Follow these steps to set grouping for the Pet Type field:

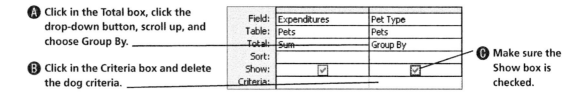

Ⓐ Click in the Total box, click the drop-down button, scroll up, and choose Group By.

Ⓑ Click in the Criteria box and delete the dog criteria.

Ⓒ Make sure the Show box is checked.

2. Run the query to produce the following recordset.

SumOfExpendit	Pet Type
$2,045.55	Cat
$2,315.55	Dog
$600.50	Rabbit

The recordset displays the total expenditures for each pet type.

3. Save the query as **Expenditures by Pet Type** then close it.

Basing a Query on Multiple Tables

You can use a query to select data from multiple tables. However, it is important that a relationship be established between the tables so the records remain synchronized. You can establish temporary relationships within the query window. However, these temporary relationships can only be used within the query. The best to way to create relationships is in the Relationships window. You used the Relationships window to create a relationship between the Customers and Pets tables in Hands-On 5.1. Relationships established within the Relationships window are then used in forms, queries, reports, and other objects dependent on the relationship.

Hands-On 5.9   Create a Multiple Table Select Query

Al Smith wants a report that lists pets and the corresponding customer information based on the last visit date of the pet. This way, his staff can contact customers if the pet has not visited the clinic recently. In this exercise, you will create a query that selects the appropriate data from the Pets and Customers tables. In Hands-On 5.11, you will use the query as the basis for a report.

The Pinnacle Pet Care database should still be open.

1. Click the Queries button on the Objects bar.

2. Double-click the Create Query in Design View option.
   The Design grid will appear and the Show Table box will be displayed.

3. Add both the Customers and Pets tables to the query window and close the Show Table box.

4. Maximize ▣ the query window.

5. Follow these steps to size the window objects and to examine the relationship:

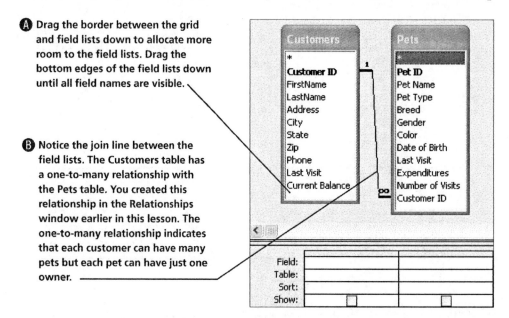

Ⓐ Drag the border between the grid and field lists down to allocate more room to the field lists. Drag the bottom edges of the field lists down until all field names are visible.

Ⓑ Notice the join line between the field lists. The Customers table has a one-to-many relationship with the Pets table. You created this relationship in the Relationships window earlier in this lesson. The one-to-many relationship indicates that each customer can have many pets but each pet can have just one owner.

6. Double-click the Last Visit field on the Pets field list (not the Customers field list) to add that field to the Design grid.

7. Now add the Pet Name and Pet Type fields from the Pets field list to the Design grid.

8. Add the Firstname, Lastname, and Phone fields from the Customers field list to the Design grid. The Design grid should contain the field names shown here.

Field:	Last Visit	Pet Name	Pet Type	FirstName	LastName	Phone
Table:	Pets	Pets	Pets	Customers	Customers	Customers
Sort:						
Show:	☑	☑	☑	☑	☑	☑
Criteria:						
or:						

9. Set the Sort key for the Last Visit field to Descending.
When you run the query, the pet with the longest absence will appear first.

Last Visit	Pet Name	Pet Type	FirstName	LastName	Phone
10/8/2003	Spike	Dog	Jacob	Samuels	(404) 367-8002
10/8/2003	Ben	Dog	Jacob	Samuels	(404) 367-8002
9/10/2003	Fetch	Dog	Jason	Jones	(415) 312-2312
9/7/2003	Bugs	Rabbit	Tony	Simpson	(510) 238-2233
9/7/2003	Max	Cat	Tony	Simpson	(510) 238-2233
7/15/2003	Wolfy	Dog	Jason	Jones	(415) 312-2312
7/15/2003	Stripes	Cat	Jason	Jones	(415) 312-2312
7/7/2003	Dillon	Dog	Mark	Roth	(510) 234-9090
7/7/2003	Tony	Cat	Mark	Roth	(510) 234-9090

10. Click the Run ![] button to produce the query results shown to the right.
Notice that the query selects every record in the Pets table and displays the corresponding customer information. The relationship ensures that the correct customer information is associated with each pet.

11. Click the Design ![] view button on the Access toolbar.
In Hands-On 5.10, you will add a pop-up box to the query. The pop-up box will prompt you to enter a date.

Parameter Queries

A parameter query displays a pop-up dialog box that prompts the user for the criteria each time it is run. You can design a parameter query to prompt for one value, or for several. For example, if you design it to prompt for two dates, Access will retrieve all data with values between those two dates. Parameter queries are useful when a query is run often but uses slightly different criteria each time. You can build a form or report on a parameter query so the user will have to provide the criteria to produce the desired recordset.

In Hands-On 5.10, you will add a criterion to the Last Visit field in the query you just created. The criterion will display a pop-up box prompting you to enter a date. The only records that will be selected when you run the query are those with a Last Visit date prior to the date you specify. This technique is quite useful because the pop-up box is also displayed when reports that are based on the query are run.

Syntax for Parameter Query Criteria

The following illustration shows the criterion that you will enter into the Last Visit field and the pop-up box that will appear. Take a few moments to study the criterion syntax.

The brackets [ ] instruct the query to display a pop-up box that prompts the user for input.

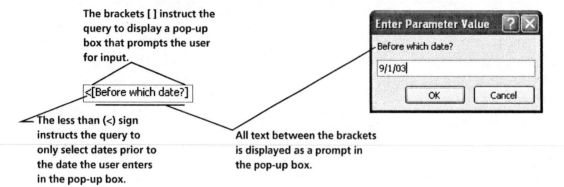

`<[Before which date?]`

The less than (<) sign instructs the query to only select dates prior to the date the user enters in the pop-up box.

All text between the brackets is displayed as a prompt in the pop-up box.

 Hands-On 5.10   Create a Pop-Up Box in a Parameter Query

In this exercise, you will add a criterion to the Last Visit field in that will display a pop-up box prompting you to enter a date. The Query Design grid should still be displayed.

1. Click in the Criteria box for the Last Visit field and enter the criteria shown here. Begin with a less than (<) sign and enclose the text in square [] brackets.

Field:	Last Visit	Pet Name	Pet Type
Table:	Pets	Pets	Pets
Sort:	Descending		
Show:	☑	☑	☑
Criteria:	<[Before which date?]		
or:			

2. Run ⚡ the query and the pop up box will appear.

3. Type **9/1/03** in the box and click OK.
   The recordset shown to the right should appear. Notice that only pets whose last visit was prior to 9/1/03 were selected.

Last Visit	Pet Name	Pet Type	FirstName	LastName	Phone
7/15/2003	Stripes	Cat	Jason	Jones	(415) 312-2312
7/15/2003	Wolfy	Dog	Jason	Jones	(415) 312-2312
7/7/2003	Dillon	Dog	Mark	Roth	(510) 234-9090
7/7/2003	Tony	Cat	Mark	Roth	(510) 234-9090

4. Choose File→Close to close the query window.

5. Click Yes when Access asks if you want to save the query.

6. Enter the name **Overdue for Visit** in the Save As box and click OK.

Query Wizards

The 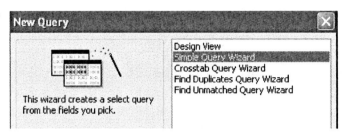 button on the Access Database toolbar displays the New Query box. The New Query box provides access to four different query wizards. The query wizards can be used as an alternative to Query Design view to set up new queries. The following table describes the various query wizards.

Query Wizards

Wizard Type	Description
Simple Query Wizard	This wizard is used to set up simple, select queries. It is usually easiest to use Query Design view to set up select queries.
Crosstab Query Wizard	This wizard creates crosstab queries used to display data in a spreadsheet-like format, with one type of data presented down the left side and the other presented across the top of the datasheet.
Find Duplicates Query Wizard	This wizard is used to locate records with duplicate field values in a table or query.
Find Unmatched Query Wizard	This wizard locates records in one table that have no related records in another table.

 Hands-On 5.11 **Use the Simple Query Wizard**

In this exercise, you will set up a simple query using the Simple Query Wizard.

1. Make sure the Queries button is chosen on the Objects bar then click the [New] button on the Access Database toolbar.

2. Choose Simple Query Wizard and click OK.
   The select query you will create will list customer names, telephone numbers, and last visit dates.

3. Choose the Customers table from the Tables/Queries list.

4. Choose the Firstname field and click the Add Field [>] button to add it to the Selected Fields list.

5. Now add the Lastname, Phone, and Last Visit fields to the Selected Fields list.

6. Click the Next button to display the second and final wizard screen.

7. Type **Last Visit Date** as the query name and click the Finish button.
   The recordset will be displayed. As you can see, it would be just as easy to set up simple queries in Query Design view. However, you may want to use the wizard to help set up queries and modify them in Design view.

8. Close the query.

Crosstab Queries

A crosstab query groups, summarizes, and arranges a recordset to make it more easily visible and with less data repetition. A crosstab query uses both row headings and column headings, displaying data in a spreadsheet format and making it easier to read and analyze. Crosstab queries calculate a Sum, Average, Count, or other type of statistic for data grouped by at least two categories. A crosstab query uses at least three fields: one as the column heading, one as the row heading, and one on which to run the statistical function. In Hands-On 5.12, you will use Pet types as the row heading and Breeds as the column heading. The statistical function will be run on Expenditures so you will get an average of the expenditures for each pet type as well as the averages of expenditures for each breed.

Pet types are listed as row headings.

Breeds are the column headings.

Pet Type	Total Of Expend	Chow	German Shephe	Jack	Mutt	Terrier	Tortoise shell	Unknown
Cat	$681.85						$450.00	$797.78
Dog	$463.11	$890.00	$397.50		$150.55	$480.00		
Rabbit	$600.50			$600.50				

The total column displays an average of expenditures for the Pet Type. We will choose the average function when we set up the query. The spreadsheet also shows averages of expenditures for each breed.

 Hands-On 5.12   Use the Query Wizard to Create a Crosstab Query

In this exercise you will set up a crosstab query based on the Pets table. This query will show the averages of expenditures by pet type.

1. Make sure the Queries button is chosen on the Objects bar then click the ⊞ New button on the Access Database toolbar.

2. Choose Crosstab Query Wizard and click OK.

3. Make sure the Tables option button is selected then click Table:Pets on which to base your crosstab query and click Next.

4. Choose the Pet type field, click the Add Field > button to add Pet Type to the Selected Fields list, and click Next
   This will be our row heading.

5. Now choose the Breed field and click Next.
   This will be our column heading.

6. Follow these steps to choose the function of this crosstab query:

Ⓐ Choose Expenditures from the Fields list.

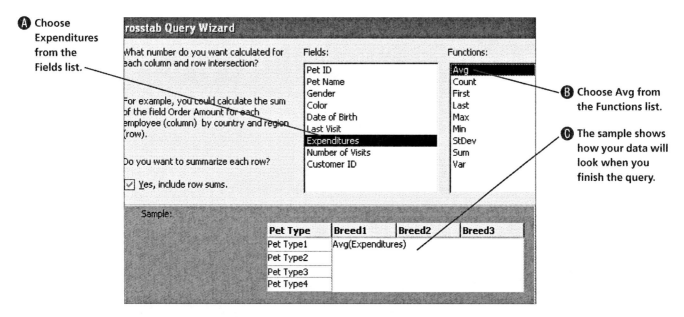

Ⓑ Choose Avg from the Functions list.

Ⓒ The sample shows how your data will look when you finish the query.

7. Click the Next button to display the final wizard screen.

8. Click Finish to accept Pets_Crosstab as the query name.

9. Follow these steps to examine the recordset:

Ⓐ Notice that the second column calculates an average of the expenditures for each Pet Type (Cat, Dog, Rabbit).

Pet Type	Total Of Expend	Chow	German Shephe	Jack	Mutt	Terrier	Tortoise shell	Unknown
Cat	$681.85						$450.00	$797.78
Dog	$463.11	$890.00	$397.50		$150.55	$480.00		
▶ Rabbit	$600.50			$600.50				

Ⓑ Notice that the remaining columns display the average expenditures for each Breed.

With a regular query you could produce a recordset that shows the average for each Breed or an average for each Pet Type, but not both at the same time. A crosstab query will allow you to see both of those averages at the same time.

10. Close the query, saving if necessary.

Action Queries

An action query usually makes changes to one or more tables. Action queries can create a new table or change an existing table by adding data to it, deleting data from it, or updating it. Because an action query is so powerful—and actually changes table data—you should consider backing up your data before running one. You can back up your tables by making copies of the ones you will be using in the query, or you can back up the entire database. The four types of action queries are:

- Delete—Deletes a group of records from one or more tables
- Update—Makes changes to records in one or more tables
- Append—Adds records to the end of one or more tables
- Make Table—Creates a new table from the records in one or more tables

To begin an action query, create a new query, or open an existing query in Design view and choose the Query Type button on the Query Design toolbar. You can use the Query Design grid to specify how you would like the data to be modified.

QUICK REFERENCE: USING ACTION QUERIES	
Task	**Procedure**
Use an action query	■ Create a new query or open the desired query in Design view.
	■ Click the Query Type button on the Query Design toolbar.
	■ Choose one of the four action queries.
	■ Set the criteria in the Design grid.
	■ Click the Datasheet view button if you want to view your results before running the query.
	■ Click the Run button on the Query Design toolbar.
	■ Accept or reject the message in the alert box. Rejecting the message cancels the action.

 Hands-On 5.13   Create a Make-Table Action Query

In this exercise, you will use the July Visits query to make a new table that will contain the records for pets that haven't been to the clinic since September 30th, 2003.

1. Make sure the Queries button is chosen on the Objects bar.

2. Choose the July Visits query and click the Design ☑ view button.
   This query uses the Pets table.

3. Click the Query Type 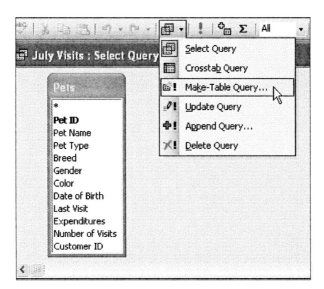 button and choose Make-Table Query, as shown here.

4. Type **Archived Pet Visits** in the Table Name box and click OK.
This will create a new table to hold the records that match the criteria you will enter next.

5. Click in the criteria box for Last Visit, remove the criteria, and type **<9/30/03**.

Field:	Pet ID	Pet Name	Pet Type	Color	Last Visit
Table:	Pets	Pets	Pets	Pets	Pets
Sort:					
Show:	☑	☑	☑	☑	☑
Criteria:					<9/30/03
or:					

6. Click the Datasheet ▦ view button to view your results.

7. Click the Design ▨ view button to go back to the Design grid.

8. Click the Run ▮ button to run the make-table query. You will see the following alert box.

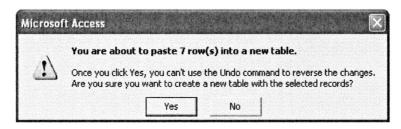

This query will copy the records that fit the criteria, adding them to the new Archived Pet Visits table. This alert box lets you know how many records will be copied.

9. Click the Yes button on the alert box to accept the action. Close the query without saving the changes.

10. Click the Tables button on the Objects bar and notice the new Archived Pet Visits table just created.

11. Double-click the Archived Pet Visits table and notice that the records all have Last Visit dates before 9/30/2003.

12. Close the Archived Pet Visits table and double-click the Pets table.
The make-table query copies the records that match the criteria from the Pets table and adds them to the new Archived Pet Visits table.

13. Close the Pets table.

Basing Reports on Queries

You can use a query as the basis for a report. This can be useful if you want the report to display data from multiple tables, or if you want the report to display only certain records from the tables. You can use the Report Wizard to create a report based on a query. The first screen in the Report Wizard lets you choose a table or query as the basis for the report.

 Hands-On 5.14 **Create a Report Based on a Query**

In this exercise, you will create a report based on a query.

1. Click the Reports button on the Objects bar in the database window.

2. Double-click the Create Report by Using Wizard option.

3. Follow these steps to choose the desired query and fields for the report:

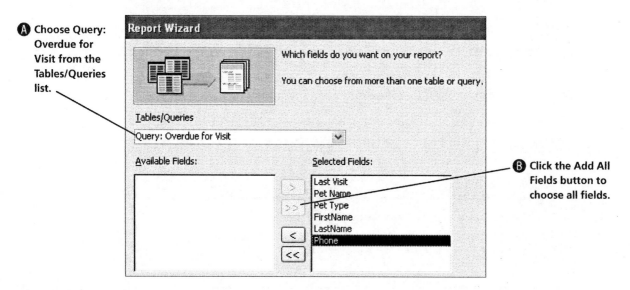

4. Click the Next button.

5. Make sure the By Pets option is chosen in the second wizard screen and click Next.
The By Pets option will base the report on the records in the Pets table. The corresponding customer information will be displayed with the pet information.

6. Click Next two more times and the Layout and Orientation options will appear.

7. Make sure the layout is set to Tabular and set the orientation to Landscape.
   Landscape orientation will set the report horizontally on the page.

8. Click Next and choose the Corporate report style.

9. Click Next and type **Overdue for Visit** as the report name in the last wizard screen.

10. Click the Finish button.
    Access will display the pop-up box prompting you to enter a date. The pop-up box appears because the report is based on the Overdue for Visit query, which contains the criterion that generates the parameter query.

11. Enter the date **9/1/03** and click OK.
    The following report should be generated.

Overdue for Visit

Last Visit	Pet Name	Pet Type	FirstName	LastName	Phone
7/15/2003	Stripes	Cat	Jason	Jones	(415) 312-2312
7/15/2003	Wolfy	Dog	Jason	Jones	(415) 312-2312
7/7/2003	Tony	Cat	Mark	Roth	(510) 234-9090
7/7/2003	Dillon	Dog	Mark	Roth	(510) 234-9090

12. Close the report then close the Pinnacle Pet Care database.

Concepts Review

True/False Questions

1. Access lets you enforce referential integrity when creating relationships. **TRUE FALSE**

2. The Zoom box is used to print recordsets. **TRUE FALSE**

3. The outcome of an action query can easily be undone. **TRUE FALSE**

4. Built-in statistical functions include Sum and Avg. **TRUE FALSE**

5. The primary purpose of the relationship is to relate a field from one table to a field of the same data type in another table. **TRUE FALSE**

6. Once you define a relationship, you cannot change it. **TRUE FALSE**

7. A parameter query is useful when the criteria are slightly different each time the query is run. **TRUE FALSE**

8. To find the largest value in a recordset, you use the Count function. **TRUE FALSE**

9. Queries can select data from multiple tables. **TRUE FALSE**

10. Pop-up boxes that prompt the user for input are created by placing criteria in the Query Design grid. **TRUE FALSE**

Multiple Choice Questions

1. Which of the following buttons is used to display the Relationships window?
   a. ⬓
   b. ⬓
   c. ⬓
   d. ⬓

2. Which pair of symbols should surround the desired phrase you want displayed in a pop-up dialog box of a parameter query?
   a. ( )
   b. [ ]
   c. < >
   d. { }

3. Which symbol(s) must be placed after the field name when creating a calculated field?
   a. :
   b. ;
   c. ( )
   d. [ ]

4. An update query _____.
   a. deletes a group of records
   b. makes a new table
   c. makes changes to a group of records
   d. moves records from one table to another

Skill Builders

Skill Builder 5.1   Establish Relationships

In this exercise, you will establish a relationship between tables in the Tropical Getaways database.

1. Open the Tropical Getaways database.

2. Click the Relationships ⛬ button on the Access toolbar.

3. Choose Customers in the Show Table box and click the Add button.
   The Customers table will be added to the Relationships window.

4. Add the Trips table and the Custom Packages table to the Relationships window then close the Show Table box.

5. If necessary, drag the bottom edges of the Customers and Trips field lists down until all field names are visible.

6. Follow these steps to establish a relationship between the Customer ID fields:

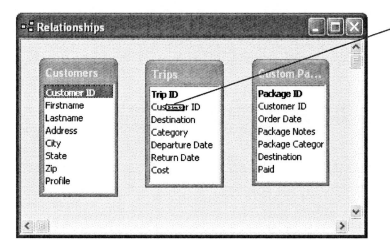

Ⓐ Drag the Customer ID field from the Customers table to the Customer ID field in the Trips table. A rectangular icon will be visible, as shown here.

Ⓑ Release the mouse button and the Edit Relationships window will appear.

7. Follow these steps to enforce referential integrity:

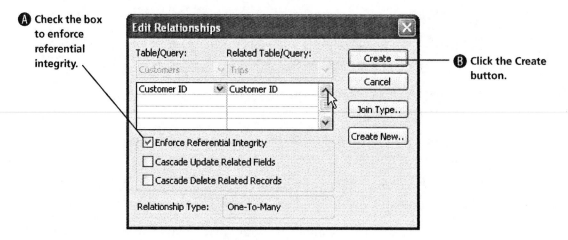

Ⓐ Check the box to enforce referential integrity.

Ⓑ Click the Create button.

Referential integrity will require that every record in the Trips table has a corresponding Customer ID in the Customers table.

8. Follow these steps to establish a relationship between the Custom Packages table and the Customers table:

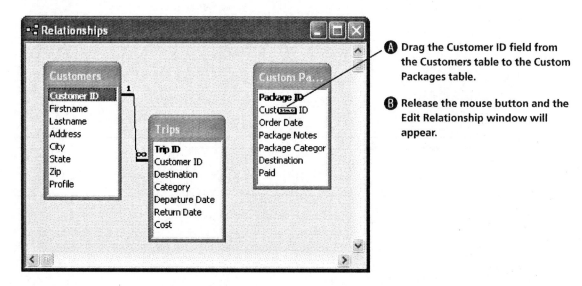

Ⓐ Drag the Customer ID field from the Customers table to the Custom Packages table.

Ⓑ Release the mouse button and the Edit Relationship window will appear.

9. Check the Enforce Referential Integrity box in the Edit Relationships window, and then click OK.

10. Click the Close [X] button at the top-right corner of the Relationships window.

11. Click Yes when Access asks if you want to save the changes to the relationship.
The relationship is now established and can be used to help you develop queries, forms, and reports.

Skill Builder 5.2   Nest Calculated Fields

In this exercise, you will use calculated fields in the Tropical Getaways database.

1. Set up a new query in Design view and add the Trips table to it.

2. Close the Show Tables dialog box.

3. Add the Destination, Category, and Cost fields to the Design grid.

4. Set the Sort box for the Category field to Ascending.

5. Follow these steps to display the Zoom box for a new calculated field:

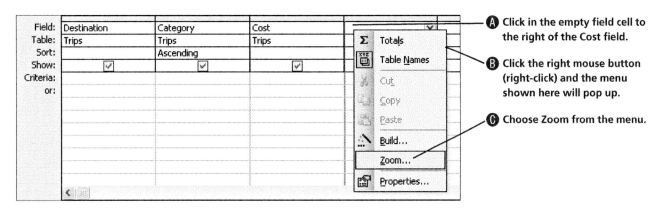

A Click in the empty field cell to the right of the Cost field.

B Click the right mouse button (right-click) and the menu shown here will pop up.

C Choose Zoom from the menu.

6. Enter the following expression into the Zoom box. Make sure you type the expression exactly as shown, including the colon after the word Duration.

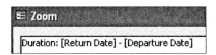

When you run the query, this expression will calculate the duration of each trip. You can perform calculations using dates in Access and Excel.

7. Click OK. Check your new calculated field for errors and correct any errors you find.

8. Run the query to produce the following recordset.

Destination	Category	Cost	Duration
Baja California	Adventu	$2,900.00	10
Rocky Mountains	Adventu	$2,190.00	16
Swiss Alps	Adventu	$3,500.00	26
Baja California	Adventu	$1,750.00	5
Amazon Jungle Trek	Adventu	$7,765.00	38
Kenyan Safari	Adventu	$6,600.00	30
Hawaii	Family	$5,300.00	8
Hawaii	Family	$3,250.00	5
Orlando	Family	$3,400.00	6
Hawaii	Leisure	$4,500.00	10
Swiss Alps	Leisure	$5,980.00	18
Caribbean Cruise	Leisure	$2,390.00	9

In the next few steps, you will add another field that calculates the average daily cost of each trip. The average daily cost will be calculated as the Cost divided by Duration. This new calculated field will use the Duration calculated field. Access allows you to nest calculated fields in this manner.

9. Switch to Design view.

10. Right-click in the empty cell to the right of the Duration cell and choose Zoom from the pop-up menu.

11. Enter the following expression into the Zoom box:

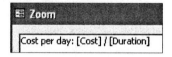

Cost per day: [Cost] / [Duration]

12. Click OK to insert the Cost Per Day calculated field into the cell.

13. Run the query to produce the following recordset.

Destination	Category	Cost	Duration	Cost per day
Baja California	Adventu	$2,900.00	10	290
Rocky Mountains	Adventu	$2,190.00	16	136.875
Swiss Alps	Adventu	$3,500.00	26	134.615384615
Baja California	Adventu	$1,750.00	5	350
Amazon Jungle Trek	Adventu	$7,765.00	38	204.342105263
Kenyan Safari	Adventu	$6,600.00	30	220
Hawaii	Family	$5,300.00	8	662.5
Hawaii	Family	$3,250.00	5	650
Orlando	Family	$3,400.00	6	566.666666667
Hawaii	Leisure	$4,500.00	10	450
Swiss Alps	Leisure	$5,980.00	18	332.222222222
Caribbean Cruise	Leisure	$2,390.00	9	265.555555556

Notice that the Cost Per Day numbers are not formatted with the Currency format. You will correct this in the next few steps.

14. Switch to Design view.

15. Right-click on the Cost Per Day field and choose Properties from the pop-up menu.

16. Click in the Format box, click the drop-down button, and choose Currency.

17. Close ▧ the Properties box.

18. Run the query. The Cost Per Day numbers should be formatted as Currency with two decimal places.

19. Close the query, and save it as **Cost Per Day**.

Skill Builder 5.3   Create a Query

In this exercise, you will set up a new query in the Tropical Getaways database. The query will select data from both the Customers and Trips tables.

1. Click the Queries button on the Objects bar in the database window.

2. Double-click the Create Query in Design view option.

3. Add both the Customers and Trips tables to the query window then close the Show Table box.

4. Maximize ▧ the Query window and adjust the size of the window objects until all field names in the Customers and Trips field lists are visible.

5. Add the Firstname and Lastname fields from the Customers field list to the Design grid.

6. Add the Destination, Category, Departure Date, Return Date, and Cost fields from the Trips field list to the grid.
   At this point, the Design grid should contain the fields shown here.

Field:	Firstname	Lastname	Destination	Category	Departure Date	Return Date	Cost
Table:	Customers	Customers	Trips	Trips	Trips	Trips	Trips
Sort:							
Show:	☑	☑	☑	☑	☑	☑	☑
Criteria:							

7. Click the Run ▯ button and the following query results should appear.

Firstname	Lastname	Destination	Category	Departure Date	Return Date	Cost
Debbie	Thomas	Kenyan Safari	Adventu	8/5/2004	9/4/2004	$6,600.00
Debbie	Thomas	Amazon Jungle Trek	Adventu	8/7/2004	9/14/2004	$7,765.00
Debbie	Thomas	Baja California	Adventu	4/17/2004	4/22/2004	$1,750.00
Debbie	Thomas	Swiss Alps	Adventu	10/10/2004	11/5/2004	$3,500.00
Wilma	Boyd	Caribbean Cruise	Leisure	9/19/2004	9/28/2004	$2,390.00
Wilma	Boyd	Swiss Alps	Leisure	5/5/2004	5/23/2004	$5,980.00
Alice	Simpson	Orlando	Family	3/4/2004	3/10/2004	$3,400.00
Alice	Simpson	Hawaii	Family	7/15/2004	7/20/2004	$3,250.00
Rita	Bailey	Rocky Mountains	Adventu	5/6/2004	5/22/2004	$2,190.00
Rita	Bailey	Baja California	Adventu	8/8/2004	8/18/2004	$2,900.00
Cheryl	DeMarco	Hawaii	Leisure	2/5/2004	2/15/2004	$4,500.00
Victor	Thomas	Hawaii	Family	3/7/2004	3/15/2004	$5,300.00

Notice that the query selects every record in the Trips table and displays the corresponding customer information.

8. Click the Design ▯ view button to return to Design view.
In the next step, you will enter a criterion in the Category criteria box. The criterion will display a pop-up box that prompts the user to enter a category. The query will only select trips with the same category type entered in the pop-up box.

9. Type the criterion **[Enter a Category]** into the Category criteria box.

Field:	Firstname	Lastname	Destination	Category
Table:	Customers	Customers	Trips	Trips
Sort:				
Show:	☑	☑	☑	☑
Criteria:				[Enter a Category]
or:				

When you run the query, the square brackets surrounding the Enter a Category phrase will instruct Access to display a pop-up box. Access will only select records where the Category is the same as the category you enter in the box. What you enter in the pop-up box must be spelled exactly as the data in the table or your recordset will be blank. If this happens, close and run the query again, making sure your spelling is correct.

10. Run ▯ the query and the pop-up box will appear.

11. Type **Adventure** in the box and click OK.
The following query results will appear. Notice that only trips with a Category of Adventure have been selected.

	Firstname	Lastname	Destination	Category	Departure Date	Return Date	Cost
	Debbie	Thomas	Kenyan Safari	Adventure	8/5/2004	9/4/2004	$6,600.00
	Debbie	Thomas	Amazon Jungle Trek	Adventure	8/7/2004	9/14/2004	$7,765.00
	Debbie	Thomas	Baja California	Adventure	4/17/2004	4/22/2004	$1,750.00
	Debbie	Thomas	Swiss Alps	Adventure	10/10/2004	11/5/2004	$3,500.00
	Rita	Bailey	Rocky Mountains	Adventure	5/6/2004	5/22/2004	$2,190.00
	Rita	Bailey	Baja California	Adventure	8/8/2004	8/18/2004	$2,900.00

12. Choose File→Close from the menu bar to close the query window.

13. Click Yes when Access asks if you want to save the query.

14. Type the name **Trips-Specific Category** in the Save As box and click OK.
In Skill Builder 5.4, you will use the query as the basis for a report.

Skill Builder 5.4   Create a Report Based on a Query

In this exercise, you will make a copy of the Trips-Specific Category query. You will modify the new query and create a new report based on the query.

1. Click the Queries button on the Objects bar in the database window.

2. Choose the Trips–Specific Category query and click the Copy ⬚ button on the Access toolbar.

3. Click the Paste ⬚ button and the Paste As box will appear.

4. Type the name **Trips–Cost Greater Than** and click OK.

5. Choose the Trips–Cost Greater Than query and click the ⬚ Design button.

6. Select [Enter a Category] in the Category criteria box and tap the [Delete] key to remove it.

7. Enter the criterion **>[Cost Greater Than]** in the Criteria box of the Cost field, as shown here.

Field:	Firstname	Lastname	Destination	Category	Departure Date	Return Date	Cost
Table:	Customers	Customers	Trips	Trips	Trips	Trips	Trips
Sort:							
Show:	☑	☑	☑	☑	☑	☑	☑
Criteria:							>[Cost Greater Than]
or:							

When the query is run, this criterion will display a pop-up box that prompts you to enter a cost. Only records where the cost is greater than what you enter will be selected.

8. Run 🔳 the query and the pop-up box will appear.

9. Type **4000** in the box and click OK.
   The following query results will appear. Notice that only trips with a cost greater than 4000 have been selected.

Firstname	Lastname	Destination	Category	Departure Date	Return Date	Cost
Debbie	Thomas	Kenyan Safari	Adventure	8/5/2004	9/4/2004	$6,600.00
Debbie	Thomas	Amazon Jungle Trek	Adventure	8/7/2004	9/14/2004	$7,765.00
Wilma	Boyd	Swiss Alps	Leisure	5/5/2004	5/23/2004	$5,980.00
Cheryl	DeMarco	Hawaii	Leisure	2/5/2004	2/15/2004	$4,500.00
Victor	Thomas	Hawaii	Family	3/7/2004	3/15/2004	$5,300.00

10. Choose File→Close from the menu bar and choose Yes to save the query changes.

11. Now use the Report Wizard and Choose the Trips–Cost Greater Than query.
    Use the fields shown in the illustration under step 16.

12. Choose the By Trips option when Access asks how you want to view the data in the second wizard screen.

13. Make sure the layout is set to Tabular and set the orientation to Landscape.

14. Click Next and choose the Soft Gray report style.

15. Click Next and enter the title **Trips by Cost**.

16. Click the Finish button.
    The following example shows the report when a cost of 4,000 is entered in the pop-up box.

Trips by Cost

Firstname	Lastname	Destination	Category	arture Date tetum Date	Cost
Debbie	Thomas	Kenyan Safari	Adventure	8/5/2004 9/4/2004	$6,600.00
Debbie	Thomas	Amazon Jungle Trek	Adventure	8/7/2004 9/14/2004	$7,765.00
Wilma	Boyd	Swiss Alps	Leisure	5/5/2004 5/23/2004	$5,980.00
Cheryl	DeMarco	Hawaii	Leisure	2/5/2004 2/15/2004	$4,500.00
Victor	Thomas	Hawaii	Family	3/7/2004 3/15/2004	$5,300.00

17. Close the report when you have finished and save any changes.

Skill Builder 5.5   Use Statistical Functions

In this exercise, you will create a query to perform statistical calculations in the Tropical Getaways database.

1. Create a new query that uses the Trips table.

2. Add the Cost field to the Design grid.

3. Display the Total row by clicking the Totals **Σ** button on the toolbar.

4. Choose the Avg function in the Total box, as shown here.

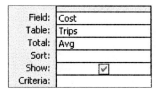

Field:	Cost
Table:	Trips
Total:	Avg
Sort:	
Show:	✓
Criteria:	

5. Run the query. The average cost of a trip should be calculated as $4,127.08.

6. Switch to Design view.

7. Add the Category field to the Design grid.
   The Total box will automatically be set to Group By. When you run the query, the Avg function in the Cost field will calculate the average cost for each Category of Trip.

Field:	Cost	Category
Table:	Trips	Trips
Total:	Avg	Group By
Sort:		
Show:	✓	✓
Criteria:		

8. Run the query to produce the following recordset.

	AvgOfCost	Category
	$4,117.50	Adventu
	$3,983.33	Family
▶	$4,290.00	Leisure

9. Close the query and save it as **Cost by Category**.

Skill Builder 5.6   Create an Update Query

In this exercise, you will create an action query that increases the cost of the trips by 10%.

1. Click the Queries button on the Objects bar in the database window.

2. Double-click the Create Query in Design view option.

3. Add the Trips table to the query window and close the Show Table box.

4. Close the Show Table box and add the Cost field.

5. Click the Query Type 🖼 ▾ button and choose Update Query.

6. Follow these steps to add 10% to the cost of the trips:

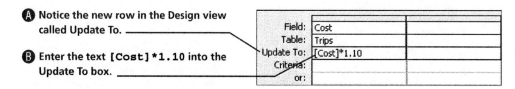

Ⓐ Notice the new row in the Design view called Update To.

Ⓑ Enter the text **[Cost]*1.10** into the Update To box.

Field:	Cost	
Table:	Trips	
Update To:	[Cost]*1.10	
Criteria:		
or:		

This will increase the cost by 10%.

7. Run the query and you will see the following alert box.

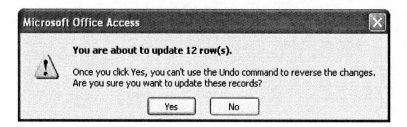

If you click Yes, you will update 12 records in the Trips table, increasing of the cost by 10%.

8. Click Yes to accept the action.

9. Click Datasheet view to see the changes in the trip costs.

Cost
$7,260.00
$8,541.50
$1,925.00
$3,850.00
$2,409.00
$3,190.00
$3,740.00
$3,575.00
$5,830.00
$2,629.00
$6,578.00
$4,950.00

This action changes the Costs in the Trips table.

10. Close the query without saving it.
You rarely save an update query. This is mainly because each time someone double-clicks the query to open it, the query will run and update the records.

Skill Builder 5.7   Create a Crosstab Query

In this exercise, you will create a crosstab query based on the Cost Per Day query to show the average cost per day for each Category of Trip as well as the average cost per day for each destination.

1. Make sure the Queries button is chosen on the Objects bar and click the [New] button.

2. Choose the Crosstab Query Wizard and click OK.

3. Make sure the Queries option button is selected, choose the Cost Per Day query, and click Next.

4. Add the Destination field to be the row heading and click Next.

5. Make sure you have the Category field as the column heading and click Next.

6. Click the Cost Per Day field and the Avg function. Your Query Wizard screen should match the following illustration.

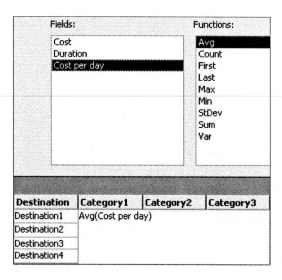

7. Click the Next button then click Finish to accept Cost per day_Crosstab as the query name. Study the following illustration to understand the query:

Destination	Total Of Cost pe	Adventure	Family	Leisure
Amazon Jungle Trek	224.776315789	224.776315789		
Baja California	352	352		
Caribbean Cruise	292.111111111			292.111111111
Hawaii	646.25		721.875	495
Kenyan Safari	242	242		
Orlando	623.333333333		623.333333333	
Rocky Mountains	150.5625	150.5625		
Swiss Alps	256.760683761	148.076923077		365.444444444

The query shows the average cost per day for each destination.

It also shows the average cost per day for each category.

8. Click the Design view button to format these numbers.
You will change the format of the numbers to currency.

9. Right-click the Cost Per Day field and choose Properties.

10. Choose Currency from the Format box.

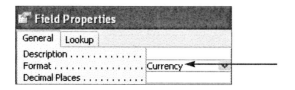

11. Format the Total Of Cost Per Day: Cost Per Day field to Currency.

12. Switch to Datasheet view to see the results.

	Destination	Total Of Cost pe	Adventure	Family	Leisure
▶	Amazon Jungle Trek	$224.78	$224.78		
	Baja California	$352.00	$352.00		
	Caribbean Cruise	$292.11			$292.11
	Hawaii	$646.25		$721.88	$495.00
	Kenyan Safari	$242.00	$242.00		
	Orlando	$623.33		$623.33	
	Rocky Mountains	$150.56	$150.56		
	Swiss Alps	$256.76	$148.08		$365.44

13. Save and close the query.

14. Close the Tropical Getaways database.

 **Assessments**

Assessment 5.1   Create a Parameter Query and Report

In this exercise, you will create a parameter query and a report based on that query to show specific models of cars in the Classic Cars database.

1. Open the Classic Cars database.

2. Create a one-to-many relationship between the Collector ID fields in the Collectors and Cars tables, as shown to the right. Enforce referential integrity then close and save the relationship.

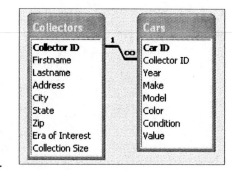

3. Create a parameter query that extracts data from the Cars and Collectors tables. The query should display a pop-up box that requests the user to enter a model. Once a model is entered, the query should only select records containing the model the user enters. The pop-up box should display the phrase **Enter a Model**. The following example assumes that the model name Corvette has been entered into the pop-up box. Assign the name **Specific Model** to the query.

Year	Make	Model	Color	Condition	Value	Firstname	Lastname
58	Chevrolet	Corvette	Red and white	Mint	$65,000.00	Cindy	Johnson
62	Chevrolet	Corvette	Blue	Excellent	$30,000.00	Tammy	Olson
58	Chevrolet	Corvette	Black	Excellent	$35,000.00	Bob	Barker
57	Chevrolet	Corvette	Red	Excellent	$42,000.00	Bob	Barker

4. Create a report based on the Specific Model query and that produces the results shown in the following illustration. The report should display the data in Landscape mode. Use the Compact report style. Assign the name **Specific Model** to the report.

Specific Model

Year	Make	Model	Color	Condition	Value	Firstname	Lastname
58	Chevrolet	Corvette	Red and white	Mint	$65,000.00	Cindy	Johnson
62	Chevrolet	Corvette	Blue	Excellent	$30,000.00	Tammy	Olson
58	Chevrolet	Corvette	Black	Excellent	$35,000.00	Bob	Barker
57	Chevrolet	Corvette	Red	Excellent	$42,000.00	Bob	Barker

5. Save and close all objects when you have finished.

Assessment 5.2   Use Statistical Functions

In this exercise, you will create a query that finds the average value of the models of cars in this table.

1. Create a new query and add the Cars table to the query.

2. Set up the query to produce the following recordset. Notice that the Model field and the Value field have been added and the average value of each model group has been calculated. The query groups the records on the Model field then calculates the average on the Value field. The query also sorts the records by Value, with the largest values appearing first.

Model	AvgOfValue
Model A	$75,000.00
Corvette	$43,000.00
Tudor	$35,000.00
Camaro	$27,500.00
Thunderbird	$20,000.00
Custom Eigh	$15,000.00
▶ Sedan	$4,900.00

3. Run the query then close and save it as **Average Value of Model Groups**.

Assessment 5.3   Create an Action Query

The staff of Classic Cars has decided to add a five dollar charge to all entrance fees to cover mailings and other costs. In this exercise, you will create an update query that adds the five dollars to the existing entrance fees.

1. Create a new query using the Events table.

2. Add the Entrance Fee field to the Design grid.

3. Create an Update query, as shown here.

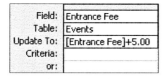

Field:	Entrance Fee
Table:	Events
Update To:	[Entrance Fee]+5.00
Criteria:	
or:	

4. Run the query, choosing Yes in the Alert box.

5. Switch to Datasheet view to see the results.

Entrance Fee
$55.00
$30.00
$15.00

The entrance fee was increased by five dollars in each record. This updates the Events table with these new values.

6. Close the query without saving it.

7. Close the Classic Cars database when you have finished then exit from Access.

Critical Thinking

Critical Thinking 5.1   Use Calculated Fields in Queries

It is important to Linda Holmes to know how much potential commission she can earn for each of her listings. Open the Holmestead Realty database and follow these guidelines to set up a query that calculates the commission for each listing:

■ Use the Listings table as the basis for the query.

■ Include the Seller ID, MLS #, Street #, Address, Price, and Commission Rate fields in the query. All of these fields should appear in the recordset in the same order shown here except for the Commission Rate field. Do not include the Commission Rate field in the recordset (but do include it in the query).

■ Create a calculated field named **Commission** that multiplies Price by Commission Rate.

■ Format the Commission calculated field with the Currency format.

■ Sort the recordset in ascending order based on the Seller ID field.

■ Save the completed query as **Commission**.

Critical Thinking 5.2   Use Statistical Functions in Queries

The broker in charge at Holmestead Realty wants to know the average price of all Linda's listings. Follow these guidelines to set up the query:

■ Create a select query that calculates the average price of Linda's listings.

■ Add a criterion that calculates the average price for Ranch style houses only.

■ Save the query as **Average Price-Ranch**.

Linda's broker would also like to see the total dollar value of listings grouped by commission rate. Follow these guidelines to set up the query:

■ The recordset should display a sum of the Price field.

■ The commission rates should be grouped and displayed in the recordset next to the sums.

■ Save your completed query as **Sum by Commission Rate**.

Critical Thinking 5.3   Create a Parameter Query

Each month, Linda would like to contact sellers who have listings that will expire that month. Follow these guidelines to set up a select query that extracts data from both the Listings and Contacts tables:

- Use the following fields in the query. The Listings table fields should appear first, followed by the Contacts table fields. All fields should follow the order shown in the table.

Listings Table	Contacts Table
Street #	FirstName
Address	LastName
Expiration Date	SpouseName
	Phone

- Enter the expression **Between [Enter First Date] and [Enter Second Date]** in the criteria box of the Expiration Date field. When the query is run, this expression will display a pop-up box that allows users to enter a date range. Any listings with an expiration date within the range you specify will appear in the recordset.

- Save the query as **Expires this Month**.

- Check the expiration dates in the Listings table then run the query using a date range that will display one or more expiration dates.

- Close Access when you are finished.

APPENDIX

Using File Storage Media

You may wish to use storage media besides the floppy disk referred to in most of the lessons. This appendix contains instructions for downloading and unzipping the exercise files used with this book, and an overview for using this book with various file storage media.

In This Appendix

The following topics are addressed in this appendix:

Downloading the Student Exercise Files

The files needed to complete certain Hands-On, Skill Builder, Assessment, and Critical Thinking exercises are available for download at the Labyrinth Website. Use the following instructions to copy the files to your computer and prepare them for use with this book.

Hands-On A.1   Download and Unzip Files

Follow these steps to download a copy of the student files necessary for this book:

1. Launch Internet Explorer.

2. Enter **labpub.com/students/fdbc2003.asp** in the browser's address bar and tap ⌈Enter⌉.
   A list of books in the applicable series appears. If you don't see the title of your book in the list, use the links on the left side of the Web page to display the list of books for your series.

3. Click the link for your book title.
   A prompt to open or save a file containing the student exercise files appears.

4. Click the Save button.

5. Choose your file storage location and click Save.
   After a pause, the exercise files will begin downloading to your computer. Continue with the next step after the download is complete.

6. Click the Open button on the Download Complete dialog box. Or, open your file storage location and double-click the newly downloaded file if the dialog box closed automatically.

7. Click OK, and then follow the step for your file storage location:
   - **Floppy Disk:** Click the Browse button, choose the $3\frac{1}{2}$ Floppy A: drive, click OK, and then click the Unzip button.
   - **USB Flash Drive:** Click the Browse button, navigate to your USB flash drive, click OK, and then click the Unzip button.
   - **My Documents Folder:** Click the Browse button, navigate to the My Documents folder, click OK, and then click the Unzip button.
   - **Network Drive Folder:** Click the Browse button, navigate to your assigned folder on the network drive, click OK, and then click the Unzip button.

8. Click the Close button after the files have unzipped.

Working with File Storage Locations

New technologies continue to expand the variety of available computer storage media. The 3½ inch floppy disk has been around since about 1983. That's incredibly ancient in the fast-moving field of computers. It's easy to use other storage media with this book. Potential alternative storage locations include:

- The My Documents folder

- A USB flash drive

- A folder on your local hard drive

- A folder on a network drive

Using Alternative File Storage Locations

Depending on the file storage media you select, some steps you perform in the exercises will differ from what you see illustrated. However, with a little practice you should find it easy to interpret the instructions for use with your file storage media.

Example: Using a USB Flash Drive

You are performing an exercise in which you create and save a new file. If you are using a USB flash drive, simply substitute the drive letter for your flash drive for the 3½ Floppy (A:) drive shown in the figure instruction.

The storage location as it appears in the book

The storage location as you perform it on the screen

Using a Floppy Disk

If you use a floppy disk to store your exercise files, you should be aware of space limitations. This section explains how to keep track of the available space on a floppy diskette, and how to delete unnecessary files to conserve space.

Storage Limitations of Floppy Disks

As you work through the exercises in this book, you will create numerous files that are to be saved to a storage location. A floppy diskette may not have enough storage capacity to hold all files created during the course (particularly if you perform all of the Skill Builder and Critical Thinking exercises). Thus, you may want to use an alternate storage location for all files accessed and created during the course.

Checking Available Space on a Floppy Disk

If you choose to use a floppy disk as your storage location, you may reach a point at which the disk fills up and no additional files can be stored on it. However, if you regularly check the available space on your floppy disk, this problem should not arise.

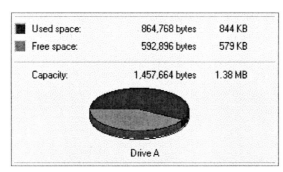

Used space:	864,768 bytes	844 KB
Free space:	592,896 bytes	579 KB
Capacity:	1,457,664 bytes	1.38 MB

Drive A

Windows can display a pie chart of the available space on your floppy disk.

Freeing Up Space on the Floppy Disk

If your floppy disk runs short of space, you will need to selectively delete files from it. You should delete files from lessons already completed, freeing up space for exercises in the current lesson.

 TIP! *Use the following procedure to check your available floppy disk space before you begin work on a new lesson. If you have less than 100 KB remaining on the disk, delete some files to free up space.*

Hands-On A.2   Check Free Space on a Floppy Disk

1. Open a My Computer window.

2. Right-click the 3½ Floppy (A:) drive and choose Properties from the context menu.
   Windows displays a pie chart with details on the used and available space on the floppy disk.

3. Examine the Free Space information and click OK.

| ■ | Used space: | 1,379,840 bytes | 1.31 MB |
| ■ | Free space: | 77,824 bytes | 76.0 KB |

4. Follow the step for the amount of disk space remaining:
   - **Close** the Properties window. Close the My Computer window if there is more than 100 KB of space remaining on the disk. Skip the remaining steps in this procedure. You are finished and ready to proceed with the next lesson.
   - **Close** ▣ the Properties window. Continue with the remaining steps in this exercise if there is less than 100 KB of space remaining on your floppy disk.

Delete Unnecessary Files

5. Double-click to open the 3½ Floppy (A:) drive.

6. Choose View→List from the menu bar.
   The My Computer window displays your files as a compact list.

7. While holding down the Ctrl key, select files for lessons that preceded the one you are working on now and tap the Delete key on the keyboard. Choose Yes if you are asked to confirm the deletion of these files.
   Windows deletes the selected files.

8. Close ▣ the My Computer window.
   You now have plenty of space for your work in the next lesson.

⚠**TIP!** *If you accidentally delete an exercise file needed for a later lesson, don't worry. You can repeat the procedure outlined in Hands-On A.1 to download and unzip the student exercise files as many times as necessary.*

■

Using a USB Flash Drive

A USB flash drive stores your data on a flash memory chip. You simply plug it into a USB port on any computer and Windows immediately recognizes it as an additional disk drive. USB flash drives typically are able store 32 megabytes (MB) or more of your data files. Large capacity USB flash drives can store 512 MB or more.

Most USB flash drives are about the size of your thumb and plug into any available USB port on your computer.

USB Flash Drive Letter

When you plug in a USB flash drive to a Windows computer, Windows automatically assigns it the next available drive letter. Windows uses drive letters to identify each drive connected to the computer. For example, the primary part of the hard drive is always identified as the C: drive. The CD/DVD drive is typically the D: or E: drive.

This USB flash drive is the F: drive.

Devices with Removable Storage

3½ Floppy (A:)   DVD/CD-RW Drive (E:)   Removable Disk (F:)

⚠️TIP! *Your USB flash drive may receive a different drive letter on different computers. This does not affect any files stored on the drive.*

Hands-On A.3   Rename Your USB Flash Drive

You may find it convenient to rename your USB flash drive to make it easier to recognize when you save or open files.

 Some Windows systems may not give you renaming privileges for drives.

1. Plug the USB flash drive into an available USB port.

2. Open a My Computer window.

3. Right-click your USB flash drive and choose Rename from the context menu.

 In the next step, Windows may display a prompt that you cannot rename this flash drive. You have not done anything wrong! You can use the drive with its current name. You may also want to try renaming it later using a different login.

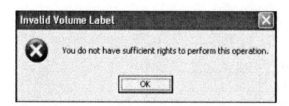

4. Type **FlashDrive** as the new drive name and tap Enter. Click OK if you receive a prompt that you do not have sufficient rights to perform this operation.
   If you were unable to rename the flash drive, don't worry. Renaming the flash drive is a convenience for recognition and has no other effect.

Using the My Documents Folder

Windows creates a unique My Documents folder for each login. This folder resides on the main system drive (usually the C: drive). The Office 2003 application programs provide a My Documents button in their Open and Save As dialog boxes to make navigation to this folder convenient.

The My Documents button in the Word 2003 Save As dialog box

Using a Network Drive Folder

You may use a system connected to a network. There may be a folder on a network server computer in another location that is dedicated to storing your work. Usually, you will find this folder within the My Network Places folder of your computer. The Office 2003 application programs provide a My Network Places button in their Open and Save As dialog boxes to make navigation to this folder convenient. You may have to navigate deeper into the folder to locate your personal network drive folder.

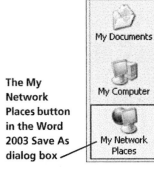

The My Network Places button in the Word 2003 Save As dialog box

Index

ISBN 1-59136-039-0

9 781591 360391